MAYER SMITH

The Illusion of Infinite Roads

Contents

1

The Forgotten Letter

The rain had started around noon, a slow, deliberate drizzle that soaked the ground and muffled the sounds of the small neighborhood. Ellie Greaves tugged her sweater tighter around her shoulders as she stood at the base of the attic stairs, staring up into the dim, cobwebbed space above. The smell of dust and damp wood wafted down, reminding her of forgotten years, of things long buried in the crevices of time.

She hadn't been up here in ages. Not since her grandmother's funeral two years ago. But today, as the rain pattered against the windows, she found herself compelled. There was no logical reason for her sudden urge to revisit the past. Perhaps it was the loneliness of her day off, or the silence that had settled over the house since her roommate moved out last month.

The attic was darker than she remembered.

Ellie hesitated, her fingers brushing against the railing. The old wood groaned beneath her touch, and she half expected something to leap out of the shadows above. Shaking her head at her own imagination, she flicked on the flashlight she had brought along and began the slow ascent.

Each step creaked underfoot, the sound sharp and accusatory in the stillness. By the time she reached the top, the air felt heavier, as if the years of memories stored here had formed an invisible weight pressing against her chest. The beam of her flashlight swept over the cluttered space, illuminating boxes stacked haphazardly, old trunks with peeling leather, and the edges of forgotten furniture draped in white sheets like ghosts waiting to be acknowledged.

Ellie set the flashlight on a wooden beam, angling it to cast its light over the area she wanted to search. Her goal was simple: to find her grandmother's recipe book. She had promised her mother she'd look for it weeks ago. Yet as she opened the first box and began sifting through yellowed papers and brittle photographs, a strange sense of unease settled over her.

The silence felt unnatural.

The rain continued to fall outside, a steady rhythm against the roof, but up here, it was too quiet. It wasn't just the absence of sound but the absence of life, as if the attic itself was holding its breath, waiting.

Ellie shoved aside a pile of ancient sewing patterns and uncovered a stack of letters tied with a faded blue ribbon. Her grandmother had always been sentimental, the kind to keep even the most trivial things. Ellie smiled faintly as she picked up the bundle. Most of the letters were addressed to her grandfather, written during his time in the war.

But one envelope caught her attention.

It was larger than the rest, its edges worn and smudged, the handwriting unfamiliar. Unlike the others, it wasn't tied with the ribbon but wedged underneath the stack, as though someone had tried to hide it. Ellie pulled it free, turning it over in her hands. There was no return address, no stamp—only her grandmother's name scrawled across the front in trembling letters.

She hesitated.

The paper felt strange, heavier than it should have been, as if its contents carried a significance she couldn't yet grasp. Her thumb brushed the seal, and she realized it had never been opened.

Curiosity clawed at her.

With careful fingers, she slid the edge of the envelope open and pulled out the letter inside. The paper was brittle, yellowed with age, and the ink had faded in places. But the words were still legible:

"Dearest Margaret,

I have no choice but to tell you the truth. By the time you read this, I will be gone. But you must understand—what happened that night wasn't an accident. The blood on my hands will never wash away, but neither will his. If you find the locket, destroy it. It carries too much pain, too much death."

The letter ended abruptly, with no signature, no explanation.

Ellie stared at it, her pulse quickening. The words swam before her eyes, the weight of their meaning sinking in slowly, like a stone dropped into a still pond. What had her grandmother been involved in? And who had written this?

The locket.

Ellie's hands trembled as she folded the letter and slipped it back into the envelope. She glanced around the attic, her heart pounding now in a way that had nothing to do with the damp chill. What locket? And what could possibly warrant such a cryptic, desperate message?

She turned back to the boxes, her movements hurried now, frantic. Papers flew in every direction as she dug through the contents, searching for anything—any clue—that could explain the letter. But the attic offered nothing but silence and shadows, as if it, too, was unwilling to give up its secrets.

The sound came suddenly.

A faint creak, like a footstep on the floorboards below.

Ellie froze, her breath hitching in her throat. The flashlight flickered, casting erratic beams across the attic. She strained to listen, her ears picking up the faintest rustle, the sound of movement.

"Hello?" she called out, her voice trembling.

No response.

She told herself it was nothing—just the house settling, or the wind pushing against the walls. But the rational part of her mind couldn't explain the sensation that followed: the undeniable feeling that she wasn't alone.

Her gaze darted to the attic door, still open at the top of the stairs. The faint glow of the hallway light below offered no comfort, only a reminder of how far she was from safety. Slowly, she reached for the flashlight and edged toward the stairs, every nerve in her body on high alert.

Another sound.

This time, it was unmistakable—a soft thud, like something heavy being dropped onto the floor below.

Ellie's throat went dry. She gripped the flashlight tighter, her knuckles white against the cold metal. The attic felt suddenly oppressive, the walls too close, the air too thin.

She forced herself to move, her steps slow and deliberate as she descended the stairs. The wooden boards groaned beneath her weight, each creak a betrayal in the silence. When she reached the bottom, she paused, peering into the dimly lit hallway.

Nothing.

But the feeling remained, that prickling at the back of her neck, the certainty that someone—or something—was there.

Her gaze flicked toward the living room. The door was slightly ajar, though she was sure she had closed it earlier. She took a hesitant step forward, the flashlight casting long, distorted shadows along the walls.

The house seemed to hold its breath.

And then she saw it.

A footprint. Wet and distinct, pressed into the hardwood floor just beyond the living room door.

Ellie's blood turned to ice. She hadn't been outside all day.

She swallowed hard, her mind racing. The letter burned in her pocket, its cryptic warning suddenly more ominous than ever. Whatever her grandmother had been hiding, it wasn't just in the past.

Someone else knew.

And now, so did she.

2

The Noisy House

The first time Ellie heard the noise, she dismissed it as the house settling. After all, the structure was old, built in the 1920s, and prone to creaks and groans that came with age. But by the third night, it had become impossible to ignore.

She was in bed when it started again, the soft knock-knock-knock echoing through the quiet house. She froze mid-scroll on her phone, her heart skipping a beat. The sound was deliberate, not the random pop of wood expanding or a draft pushing against a loose windowpane. It was coming from downstairs.

Ellie lowered her phone and listened.

The rain had returned, tapping steadily against the windows, masking some of the softer noises. But there it was again: knock-knock-knock. Slow and steady, like someone rapping their knuckles against the wall.

She slid out of bed, the hardwood floor cold beneath her

bare feet. Grabbing the heavy flashlight she had left on her nightstand, she padded to the bedroom door and cracked it open, peering into the shadowed hallway.

"Hello?" she called, her voice barely more than a whisper.

No response.

The knock came again, louder this time, more insistent.

Ellie's breath caught. Her mind raced through possibilities: A tree branch brushing against the side of the house? A bird caught under the eaves? Or something else, something her rational mind didn't want to entertain.

She moved toward the stairs, her hand trailing along the banister for balance. The house was eerily quiet except for the rain and the persistent knock, which seemed to be coming from the kitchen.

As she descended, the flashlight's beam swept over the familiar shapes of the living room: the sagging sofa, the outdated TV, the coffee table littered with unopened mail. Everything looked as it should. Normal. But the air felt different, charged, as though the house itself was waiting for something.

The knocking stopped the moment her foot touched the bottom step.

Ellie froze, gripping the flashlight tighter. The silence was deafening now, the absence of the sound almost more unnerving than its presence.

"Is someone there?" she asked, her voice firmer this time.

Nothing.

Summoning her courage, she moved toward the kitchen. The flashlight's beam flicked across the countertops, the sink, the fridge. The room was empty, just as she'd left it. But the uneasy feeling lingered, the sensation that she was being watched.

A sudden crash shattered the silence, coming from the direction of the dining room. Ellie gasped, nearly dropping the flashlight. Her pulse thundered in her ears as she spun toward the sound.

The dining room door was ajar, the darkness beyond it thick and impenetrable.

She hesitated, every instinct screaming at her to turn back, to lock herself in her room and wait for morning. But the crash had sounded real, tangible—a chair overturned, or a plate shattered. She had to know what it was.

With trembling hands, she pushed the door open and stepped inside. The flashlight's beam cut through the darkness, revealing the long wooden table, the mismatched chairs, the dusty chandelier overhead. Everything appeared undisturbed.

Then she saw it: a single chair pushed away from the table, lying on its side.

Her breath hitched. She hadn't been in the dining room for days, hadn't touched the chairs since her roommate moved out.

"Who's there?" she demanded, her voice shaking.

The room answered with silence.

Ellie approached the fallen chair cautiously, her flashlight sweeping the floor around it. There was no sign of movement, no indication of who—or what—had knocked it over. But as she bent to right the chair, the knocking resumed.

This time, it was coming from upstairs.

She shot upright, the chair forgotten. The sound was louder now, echoing through the house in a steady rhythm: knock-knock-knock.

Her stomach twisted. She had been upstairs just minutes ago, had seen with her own eyes that the hallway and bedrooms were empty. Yet the noise was unmistakable, coming from the direction of her room.

Clutching the flashlight like a weapon, Ellie backed out of the dining room and made her way to the stairs. Each step felt heavier than the last, her legs trembling beneath her.

The knocking continued, relentless, as though daring her to confront it.

When she reached the top of the stairs, she paused, her flash-light aimed down the hallway. The door to her room was ajar, the faintest sliver of light spilling into the corridor.

She hadn't left it like that.

"Whoever you are, you need to leave," Ellie said, forcing as much authority into her voice as she could muster.

The knocking stopped.

Her pulse hammered in the silence that followed, her throat dry as sandpaper. She stepped closer to the door, her breath hitching with every movement. The flashlight's beam wavered slightly, betraying the unsteadiness of her hands.

When she reached the doorway, she hesitated. The room beyond was still, the familiar shapes of her bed and dresser casting long shadows against the walls.

She stepped inside.

The room was exactly as she had left it—except for one thing.

The envelope.

It was lying on her bed, the same envelope she had found in the attic earlier that week. She had left it on the kitchen counter, intending to show it to her mother. But now, here it was, the letter spilling out of its slit seal as though someone had been reading it.

Ellie approached cautiously, her heart pounding. She picked up the envelope and turned it over in her hands. The paper felt colder than before, damp, as though it had been outside in the rain.

A soft creak behind her sent her spinning around, the flashlight's beam slicing through the room.

The closet door, which had been firmly closed, was now ajar.

Her breath caught in her throat.

Ellie took a step back, her mind racing. Had it always been open, and she simply hadn't noticed? Or had someone—or something—opened it while she was focused on the letter?

The rain outside intensified, the wind howling against the windows. Ellie's grip on the flashlight tightened as she moved toward the closet, each step slow and deliberate.

"Is someone in there?" she asked, her voice cracking.

The closet didn't respond, but the unease in the air seemed to grow heavier, pressing down on her like an invisible weight.

She reached out with her free hand, her fingers trembling as they brushed against the edge of the door. With a quick motion, she flung it open and stepped back, her flashlight illuminating the space inside.

It was empty.

Her clothes hung neatly on their hangers, the floor bare except for a pair of shoes. There was no sign of an intruder, no explanation for the noise or the open door.

And then she noticed it.

On the floor of the closet, barely visible in the dim light, was a single, muddy footprint.

Ellie stumbled back, her chest tightening with panic. The footprint was fresh, the mud still wet, and it was far too large to be her own.

She turned and fled the room, her flashlight beam bouncing wildly as she raced down the hallway. The knocking started again, louder this time, echoing from every corner of the house.

It followed her as she bolted down the stairs and into the living room, her heart hammering in her chest. She didn't stop until she reached the front door, her fingers fumbling with the lock.

The moment she stepped outside, the knocking stopped.

The house loomed behind her, silent and dark, the rain washing over its ancient walls. Ellie stood on the porch, her breath coming in ragged gasps, the envelope clutched tightly in her hand.

Somewhere inside, she knew, the house was waiting.

3

The Locked Room

The call came in just after dawn, interrupting the steady rhythm of Detective Caleb Hart's morning coffee. He'd been staring at the skyline from his tenth-floor apartment, letting the silence settle around him, when his phone buzzed insistently on the counter. The number on the screen was familiar—the station— but the clipped tone of the officer on the other end was anything but routine.

"Detective Hart? We've got a situation at the Armitage estate. It's... unusual. You're going to want to see this."

"Define 'unusual,'" Caleb asked, already reaching for his coat.

There was a pause on the line, then: "A locked room. One body. No sign of entry or exit."

—-

The Armitage estate loomed ahead like a relic from another era, its gothic spires reaching toward the gray morning sky. The mansion sat at the end of a long, winding driveway, flanked by ancient oaks that swayed under the weight of the cold autumn wind. The air smelled of damp earth and decay, the kind of scent that clung to old places steeped in history and secrets.

Caleb stepped out of his car and adjusted his collar against the chill. A uniformed officer approached, his face pale and drawn.

"Detective," the officer said, nodding. "The scene's upstairs. Third floor. Master bedroom."

"What's the story?" Caleb asked as they ascended the grand staircase, his boots echoing against the polished wood.

"Mrs. Armitage found him—her husband, Charles—this morning. She said the room was locked from the inside. We had to break it down to get in. No other entrances, no windows opened, no sign of anyone else in there."

Caleb frowned. "Cause of death?"

The officer hesitated. "That's where it gets... strange. You'll see."

They reached the third floor, where the hallway stretched long and narrow, lined with antique portraits whose painted eyes seemed to follow Caleb's every move. The door to the master bedroom stood ajar, the lock splintered from the force of the breach. Beyond it, the room waited, still and heavy with an atmosphere Caleb could only describe as wrong.

He stepped inside.

The master bedroom was grand, dominated by a massive four-poster bed draped in rich burgundy fabric. The air was thick, carrying the faint metallic tang of blood. Caleb's eyes were immediately drawn to the figure sprawled on the rug in the center of the room.

Charles Armitage lay on his back, his lifeless eyes staring at the ornate ceiling. His hands were clenched into fists, his face frozen in an expression of sheer terror. A deep gash ran across his throat, the blood pooling beneath him stark against the light-colored rug.

Caleb crouched beside the body, careful not to disturb anything. The cut was clean, precise, not the work of someone in a frenzy.

"What about the windows?" he asked without looking up.

"Locked," the officer replied. "From the inside. We checked them twice. No tampering, no footprints outside."

Caleb's gaze shifted to the nearest window. The latch was indeed secured, the glass untouched by smudges or condensation. He stood and scanned the rest of the room. A single chair sat near the fireplace, a book left open on its armrest. The bed was undisturbed, the covers neatly arranged.

No signs of a struggle. No weapon.

"How long has he been dead?"

"The medical examiner's on her way, but from the state of the blood…" The officer glanced at the body, his discomfort evident. "Probably a few hours. Mrs. Armitage says she last saw him alive around midnight. She found him when she tried to bring him coffee this morning."

Caleb turned toward the door. "And where is Mrs. Armitage now?"

"Downstairs in the sitting room. Shaken, but cooperative."

"I'll speak to her shortly," Caleb said. His focus returned to the room, his mind working through the possibilities.

A locked room was always a puzzle. But this one felt different—darker. There was something off about the air, a weight that pressed down on him the longer he stood there.

He stepped toward the fireplace, examining the open book. It was an old volume, its leather cover worn and cracked. The text inside was in Latin, the words faded but still legible. Caleb's Latin was rusty, but one phrase stood out, repeated several times on the visible pages: Clavis ex tenebris—"Key from the darkness."

"What the hell were you reading, Charles?" he muttered.

As he turned back to the body, something caught his eye—a faint marking on the floorboards near the edge of the rug. He crouched for a closer look.

It was a symbol, carved lightly into the wood. A circle intersected by a series of jagged lines, its edges blackened as though burned.

"Did anyone notice this?" Caleb asked, gesturing toward the symbol.

The officer frowned. "No, sir. I don't think anyone's seen it yet."

Caleb's unease deepened. The symbol didn't look like it belonged in a modern home; it was older, almost ritualistic.

"Make sure this is documented," he said. "Every detail."

—-

Mrs. Armitage was waiting for him in the sitting room, her hands clasped tightly around a porcelain teacup. She was in her late fifties, her face pale and drawn but composed.

"Mrs. Armitage," Caleb began as he took a seat across from her. "I know this is a difficult time, but I need to ask you some questions about your husband."

She nodded stiffly. "Of course, Detective. I'll do my best."

"When was the last time you saw Charles?"

"Just before midnight," she said. "He'd come up to bed, but he said he wanted to read for a while. I went to sleep. When I woke up this morning, I realized he hadn't come down, so I went to check on him."

"Did you hear anything unusual during the night?"

"No," she said quickly, then hesitated. "Well... there was a sound. Around three in the morning, I think. It was faint, like... like scratching. I thought it was just the wind."

"Scratching," Caleb repeated. "From where?"

"I don't know. It seemed to be coming from everywhere."

Her words sent a chill through him. He leaned forward slightly. "Did your husband ever mention anything unusual? Any threats, anything that might explain what happened?"

She shook her head. "No. But..." She hesitated, her fingers tightening around the teacup. "He's been... different lately. Restless. He kept talking about a 'key.' Said he had to find it, that it would fix everything. I thought he was just stressed. Work had been difficult lately."

Caleb's mind immediately went to the phrase in the book upstairs: Key from the darkness.

"What kind of work did Charles do?"

"He was a historian," she said. "He specialized in... obscure artifacts, ancient texts. He was always fascinated by things that others overlooked."

Obscure artifacts. Ancient texts. Caleb's thoughts returned to the symbol carved into the floor, the strange phrase in the book.

"Mrs. Armitage," he said carefully, "did your husband ever mention the name 'Clavis ex tenebris'?"

Her face went pale. The teacup trembled in her hands.

"Yes," she whispered. "He said it was important. That it was the key he'd been looking for."

Caleb's unease solidified into a gnawing sense of dread. Whatever had happened in that locked room wasn't just a crime. It was something much more sinister.

And he had the sinking feeling that the answers he sought would only lead to more questions.

4

The Missing Memory

The first thing Ethan Monroe noticed when he woke up was the silence. Not the kind of silence that comes with the early morning or an empty house, but an oppressive quiet that seemed to press against his skull, muffling his thoughts and senses.

He was lying on a cold, hard surface. As his eyes fluttered open, he realized it wasn't his bed or even the familiar texture of his couch beneath him. No, this was concrete—cold, unyielding, and dusted with dirt that clung to his skin.

Where am I?

The question thundered through his mind as he pushed himself upright. His head throbbed with a sharp, pulsing pain that made him wince. His palms scraped against the rough floor, and as he looked around, his breath caught.

The room was dimly lit, the faint glow of a single bulb swinging from the ceiling casting jagged shadows across the walls. It was bare except for a battered wooden chair in the corner and a broken mirror leaning against one wall. The air smelled of mildew and something faintly metallic.

Ethan's heart began to race. How did I get here?

His memories were fragments, pieces of a puzzle that didn't fit. He remembered going to bed—he was sure of it. He had been in his apartment, the soft hum of his refrigerator lulling him to sleep. Then... nothing.

His fingers brushed against something cold on the floor. He looked down and saw a small metal object—a key. It was old, its surface tarnished, with an intricate design etched into its bow.

A key? To what?

He pocketed it instinctively, his mind racing. He stood, unsteady at first, and approached the door. It was heavy, reinforced metal, and when he tried the handle, it didn't budge. A quick glance at the keyhole confirmed his suspicion—the key didn't fit.

Panic began to claw at the edges of his mind. He turned toward the mirror, his reflection distorted by the cracked glass. He barely recognized himself. His dark hair was disheveled, his shirt wrinkled and stained with something he couldn't identify. And then he saw it—a streak of crimson along his forearm.

Blood.

His stomach churned. He rolled up his sleeve, revealing a long, shallow cut. It wasn't deep, but it was enough to send his mind spiraling. Whose blood is this?

As he stared at the wound, something else caught his attention—a faint series of numbers scrawled on the inside of his wrist, as though written hastily with a marker:

3:15 AM

What does it mean?

A sudden noise jolted him from his thoughts. It was faint, a soft creak, but in the oppressive silence, it sounded deafening. Ethan's head whipped toward the door. Someone was out there.

"Hello?" His voice cracked, dry and hoarse. He tried again, louder. "Who's there?"

No response.

The creak came again, followed by the faint sound of footsteps. Whoever—or whatever—was out there wasn't in a hurry. The measured pace of the steps sent a shiver down his spine.

He scanned the room, looking for something, anything he could use as a weapon. His eyes landed on the broken leg of the chair in the corner. He rushed toward it, his movements frantic, and yanked it free.

Armed with his makeshift weapon, Ethan positioned himself near the door, his pulse pounding in his ears. The footsteps grew louder, then stopped.

The silence returned, heavier this time, suffocating.

The doorknob rattled.

Ethan's grip on the chair leg tightened. His breath came in short, shallow bursts as the rattling turned into a slow, deliberate scraping sound.

Then, without warning, the noise stopped.

Ethan waited, every muscle in his body tense. Seconds passed, stretching into what felt like an eternity. Finally, he mustered the courage to call out again.

"Whoever's out there, I swear I'll—"

The bulb above him flickered and went out, plunging the room into darkness.

Ethan froze, his breath hitching in his throat. He couldn't see a thing, but he could feel the air around him change, as though he wasn't alone anymore.

A soft whisper broke the silence, so faint he almost missed it.

"Ethan..."

His name, spoken with a rasping, otherworldly quality. He spun around, his weapon raised, but there was nothing there.

The whisper came again, closer this time.

"Ethan... why?"

"Why what?" he shouted, his voice cracking. "What do you want from me?"

The bulb sputtered back to life, casting the room in its dim glow once more. Ethan blinked, his eyes adjusting, and then he saw it—something scrawled on the wall in thick, dripping letters.

WHERE IS SHE?

His heart stopped. The words hadn't been there before.

"Who?" he demanded, his voice shaking. "Who are you talking about?"

No answer.

The door creaked open, just an inch, enough to reveal a sliver of the hallway beyond. Ethan hesitated, his instincts screaming at him to stay put, but he couldn't ignore the pull of curiosity—or the desperation to escape.

He approached the door cautiously, his weapon raised. The hallway was dim, lined with peeling wallpaper and flickering sconces. It stretched in both directions, empty and endless.

Ethan stepped out, his footsteps echoing. He turned left, the key in his pocket pressing against his leg with every step.

As he moved, fragments of memory began to surface—flashes of a woman's face, her eyes wide with fear; the sound of muffled screams; the weight of something heavy in his hands.

"No," he whispered to himself. "That's not real. It can't be real."

The hallway twisted and turned, leading him deeper into the labyrinth. The air grew colder, the walls closing in. Just as he was about to turn back, he spotted something ahead—a door, slightly ajar.

He approached it, his heartbeat loud in his ears. Pushing the door open, he found himself in another room, almost identical to the one he'd woken up in.

Except this one wasn't empty.

In the center of the room was a chair, and in the chair sat a woman. Her head was slumped forward, her long hair obscuring her face. Her hands were bound to the armrests with thick ropes.

"Hello?" Ethan said, his voice trembling.

She didn't respond.

He stepped closer, his stomach churning. "Miss? Are you

okay?"

No answer.

Ethan reached out, his hand trembling, and gently lifted her chin.

Her face was pale, her lips blue. Her lifeless eyes stared back at him, wide and unseeing.

Ethan staggered back, his mind reeling. He didn't recognize her, but the sight of her filled him with an overwhelming sense of guilt.

His eyes darted to her wrist. There, scrawled in the same marker as his own, were the numbers 3:15 AM.

"What's happening?" he whispered, his voice breaking.

Behind him, the door slammed shut.

Ethan whirled around, his weapon raised, but there was no one there.

And then he heard it again—the whisper.

"Ethan... you know."

He sank to his knees, his hands clutching his head as the fragments of memory pieced themselves together. The woman's face, her screams, the weight of the key in his pocket.

He had been here before.

And he had done something unforgivable.

5

The Secret Passenger

The rain pelted against the windshield in heavy sheets, the wipers struggling to keep up as they swished rhythmically back and forth. The dark highway stretched endlessly ahead, illuminated only by the twin beams of the car's headlights. Claire adjusted her grip on the steering wheel, her knuckles white with tension. The radio crackled with static, the last remnants of a forgotten station fading as she drove deeper into the rural backroads.

This wasn't her first long drive, but something about this one felt... off. Maybe it was the storm, or the isolation, or the unease that had been gnawing at her ever since she passed the last gas station miles ago. The attendant had given her a strange look when she mentioned where she was headed.

"Not much out that way," he had said, his tone more warning than observation.

Claire had laughed it off at the time. Now, as the shadows

pressed in on her from the edges of the road, she wasn't so sure.

The GPS on her phone chirped, the robotic voice breaking the silence. "Continue straight for 27 miles."

"Great," she muttered, her voice barely audible over the drumming of the rain. Twenty-seven more miles of nothingness. She glanced at the clock on the dashboard—1:13 AM. She should've been home hours ago, but the detour had added an unexpected delay.

She was reaching for her water bottle when she saw it—a flash of movement in her peripheral vision. Her heart skipped a beat, and her eyes darted to the rearview mirror. For a moment, she thought she saw a figure in the backseat, but it was gone as quickly as it appeared.

Just a trick of the light, she told herself, forcing her gaze back to the road. Shadows played tricks in storms like this, especially when you were tired. Still, she couldn't shake the feeling that she wasn't alone.

The car's engine hummed steadily as the rain continued to pour. Claire's grip tightened on the wheel again, her eyes flicking to the mirror more often now. Each time, the backseat stared back at her, empty and shadowed. But the feeling of being watched persisted, growing stronger with every passing mile.

She turned on the radio, desperate for some noise to fill the void. Static greeted her again, followed by faint snippets of a song before it dissolved back into nothingness. She sighed, turning the knob in search of a station. As she did, the rearview mirror caught her eye again.

This time, she froze.

There was no mistaking it now. A shape was there, faint and indistinct, seated in the middle of the backseat. Her breath hitched, and the car swerved slightly as her hands faltered on the wheel. She snapped her gaze forward, her pulse hammering in her ears.

"It's nothing," she whispered to herself. "Just your imagination."

But it didn't feel like her imagination.

Claire's hands trembled as she glanced at the mirror again. The shape was still there, and this time it seemed... closer. She couldn't make out any features—just the suggestion of a head and shoulders, outlined faintly in the gloom. Her chest tightened, and she forced her eyes back to the road.

"Okay," she said aloud, her voice shaking. "Just stay calm. It's not real. You're tired, and the storm is messing with your head."

The GPS interrupted her thoughts again. "In one mile, turn left onto Ridgewood Road."

Claire exhaled shakily, grateful for the distraction. She focused on the road ahead, ignoring the mirror. When the turn came into view, she flicked on her signal and eased the car onto the narrower, winding road.

The rain seemed to intensify as she drove, the sound of it pounding on the roof almost deafening. The road was darker here, the trees on either side forming a tunnel that swallowed the headlights. Claire's unease deepened. She couldn't help but steal another glance at the mirror.

This time, the shape was unmistakably human.

A gasp escaped her lips as her eyes locked on the figure. It was sitting perfectly still, its head tilted slightly as though watching her. Panic surged through her, and she nearly slammed on the brakes. Instead, she forced herself to keep driving, her hands shaking so badly she could barely keep the car steady.

"Who's there?" she shouted, her voice trembling. She didn't expect an answer, but the silence that followed was even worse.

Her mind raced. Did someone get into the car while she was at the gas station? How could she not have noticed? And why weren't they saying anything?

Her breathing quickened, and she gripped the wheel so tightly her fingers ached. She needed to stop, to pull over and figure out what was happening. But the thought of stopping on this desolate road with a stranger—an intruder—behind her was even more terrifying.

She glanced at the mirror again, unable to help herself. The figure hadn't moved, but its presence was suffocating. Claire's throat tightened as a memory surfaced, unbidden.

A news story she'd heard a few weeks ago, about a woman driving alone late at night. She'd stopped for gas, and when she got back on the road, she'd noticed something strange—someone in her backseat. By the time she realized, it was too late.

"No," Claire whispered. "No, no, no."

She needed to think. She needed to stay calm. But her mind was a whirlwind of fear and confusion. Her eyes darted to the clock—1:27 AM. She still had miles to go, and the rain showed no sign of letting up.

The GPS broke the silence once more. "Continue straight for five miles."

Claire's heart sank. She couldn't take five more miles of this. She had to do something. Her phone was in the cupholder, but the thought of reaching for it, of taking her eyes off the road—or the mirror—was unbearable.

"Who are you?" she demanded, her voice cracking. "What do you want?"

The figure didn't respond. It didn't move.

Claire's frustration and fear boiled over, and she slammed her hand on the steering wheel. "Say something!"

The sound of her voice echoed in the car, followed by a deafening crack of thunder. The lights flickered, and for a terrifying moment, the car was plunged into darkness. When the headlights returned, the road was empty, but Claire's focus was no longer on the road.

It was on the mirror.

The figure had vanished.

Relief washed over her, but it was fleeting. Her hands shook as she drove, her eyes darting from the mirror to the road and back again. Had she imagined it? Was it really gone? Or was this some cruel trick?

The rain began to let up, the storm finally easing. The GPS announced her next turn, and she took it, the winding road giving way to a straighter path. Her tension didn't ease, though. If anything, it grew sharper, more acute.

She glanced at the mirror one last time.

The backseat was empty.

But as Claire exhaled, her relief was shattered. From the corner of her eye, she saw it—not in the mirror, but beside her. A shadowy figure, seated in the passenger seat, its face turned toward hers.

A scream tore from her throat, and the car swerved violently. She fought for control, her heart pounding as she slammed on the brakes. The car skidded to a stop, the engine sputtering before falling silent.

When she finally dared to look, the passenger seat was empty.

Claire sat there in the silence, the rain dripping from the roof, her chest heaving with ragged breaths. She didn't dare move. Didn't dare speak.

And then, from somewhere behind her, came a faint, chilling whisper.

"Don't stop."

6

The Vanishing Footprints

The snow fell in thick, silent flakes, covering the forest in a pristine white blanket. It was the kind of stillness that made the world feel untouched, as if no one had ever walked these trails before. Thomas pulled his scarf tighter around his neck and adjusted his headlamp, its beam cutting through the falling snow.

The woods seemed alive with shadows, the trees stretching their dark limbs toward the sky. He hadn't meant to wander so far, but the argument with his father earlier that evening had driven him out of the house. With each angry step, he had let the forest pull him deeper into its embrace, the sound of his boots crunching on the fresh snow echoing in the emptiness.

The fight played on a loop in his mind. His father, red-faced and shouting, accusing Thomas of being irresponsible, unmotivated, and unwilling to face his future. The words had stung more than Thomas wanted to admit. He had stormed out, grabbing his coat and boots without a word, determined to put as much distance as possible between himself and his father's disappointment.

Now, miles from home, the forest seemed to mock his anger. The storm had picked up, and the snow was falling faster, the wind biting at his face. He paused, realizing he couldn't remember exactly which direction he had come from. Turning in a slow circle, he scanned the forest for any sign of a familiar landmark, but the trees all looked the same.

His breath formed clouds in the freezing air, and for the first time, a flicker of unease crept into his thoughts. He was a seasoned hiker and knew these woods well—or so he thought. But now, in the middle of a snowstorm, everything felt unfamiliar.

Thomas decided to follow his own footprints back. Turning toward the trail he had made, he felt a rush of relief seeing the clear indentations of his boots in the snow. The tracks stretched out behind him in a winding path, leading back the way he had come.

But as he began retracing his steps, something caught his eye.

About twenty feet back, just where the curve of his trail should have been, the footprints stopped.

He froze, his breath catching in his throat. The tracks didn't veer off to the side or disappear into the underbrush. They simply... ended. A perfect line of prints, clear and deep, abruptly cut off as if he had vanished into thin air mid-step.

Thomas swallowed hard, his pulse quickening. He turned his headlamp toward the area around the trail. The snow was unbroken, smooth and untouched. There were no signs of animal tracks, no disturbances in the pristine surface. The wind, though biting, wasn't strong enough to completely erase footprints, especially not so suddenly.

A chill ran down his spine, one that had nothing to do with the cold. He forced himself to take a step forward, then another, until he was standing at the edge of his own vanished trail. Bending down, he inspected the snow. The last print was sharp and detailed, the edges crisp. But beyond it, the snow was completely undisturbed.

"Maybe I made a wrong turn," he muttered to himself, though the words sounded hollow. He glanced around again, scanning the forest for any sign of movement. The snow muffled all sound, leaving the woods eerily quiet. His headlamp's beam bounced across the trees, casting long, flickering shadows.

But he was alone. At least, that's what he told himself.

Thomas turned back to the trail ahead of him, now walking more quickly. He would find another set of tracks, he thought. Maybe he had looped around without realizing it. Maybe the snow was playing tricks on his eyes.

But as he walked, the unease gnawed at him. Every few steps, he glanced over his shoulder, certain he would see something—or someone—following him. The forest felt alive, watching.

And then he saw them.

New footprints.

They weren't his.

Thomas stopped, his heart pounding in his chest. The prints were fresh, their edges sharp, leading directly across his path. They were small, as if made by a child, and they seemed to come from nowhere, starting in the middle of the trail and heading deeper into the woods.

"Hello?" he called, his voice echoing through the trees. It felt wrong to speak, as though he were breaking some unspoken rule. The sound of his own voice only heightened his sense of isolation.

There was no answer. Only the whisper of the wind and the soft hiss of snow falling.

Against his better judgment, Thomas followed the strange footprints. They weaved through the trees in an erratic pattern, as if whoever made them was wandering aimlessly. He told himself he was being practical. If someone was lost out here, he needed to help them. But deep down, he wasn't sure that was the truth.

The prints continued for about fifty feet before they, too, vanished.

Thomas stared at the empty snow where the trail ended. It was the same as before—no signs of disturbance, no indication of where the person might have gone. He felt the hair on the back of his neck rise, a deep, primal fear taking hold.

"Who's there?" he called again, louder this time. His voice cracked, betraying his fear.

Still, there was no reply.

He turned in a slow circle, scanning the forest. His headlamp caught the flash of something in the distance—a faint, fleeting movement, just beyond the reach of the light. His breath hitched, and he took an involuntary step back.

"Hey!" he shouted. "If you're out there, show yourself!"

The silence that followed was deafening.

Then he heard it.

A faint sound, almost imperceptible over the wind—a soft crunching of snow. It was coming from behind him. Slowly, he turned, his headlamp sweeping across the trees.

Nothing.

The sound came again, closer this time. Thomas's chest tightened, and he gripped the straps of his backpack as if they could anchor him. "Who's there?" he demanded, his voice shaking.

The crunching stopped.

And then, as if mocking him, a single footprint appeared in the snow just a few feet away from where he stood.

Thomas stumbled back, his heart racing. His headlamp flickered, plunging him into momentary darkness before the light returned. When it did, the footprint was gone.

He broke into a run, his boots slipping on the icy ground as he tried to put as much distance as possible between himself and... whatever this was. His breath came in ragged gasps, each exhale a plume of vapor in the freezing air. The forest seemed to close in around him, the trees pressing closer, their shadows stretching like grasping hands.

He didn't stop until he saw his own house through the trees, its warm lights glowing faintly in the distance. Relief washed over him, but it was short-lived. As he reached the edge of the woods, he glanced back one last time.

The footprints were there, a single trail leading directly to where he stood.

And then, as he watched, they vanished. One by one, as if erased by an unseen hand, until the snow was pristine once more.

7

The Silent Phone

The phone buzzed violently on the nightstand, jolting Rachel awake. Her eyes flicked to the glowing red digits on her alarm clock—2:12 AM. She groaned, reaching blindly for the phone, her fingers fumbling in the darkness. Who would be calling her at this hour? The number on the screen was unknown, but curiosity and irritation compelled her to swipe the screen.

"Hello?" she mumbled, her voice thick with sleep.

There was no answer, just silence.

"Hello?" she repeated, sitting up now, her annoyance rising. The faint crackle of static whispered in her ear, like the distant hum of an old radio. Then, just as she was about to hang up, a voice—barely audible—broke through.

"Rachel..."

The single word sent a chill down her spine. The voice was distorted, like it was coming from underwater, but it unmistakably said her name.

"Who is this?" she demanded, her pulse quickening.

The line went dead.

Rachel stared at the phone, her heart thudding in her chest. She checked the number again, hoping it was just some prank call. The number was untraceable—just a series of zeros. She tossed the phone onto the bed and ran her hands through her hair, willing herself to calm down.

"It's nothing," she muttered aloud. "Probably just some weirdo."

But as she lay back down, the unease lingered, curling around her like a fog.

— -

The following day passed uneventfully. By evening, Rachel had managed to convince herself that the call was a glitch, or perhaps a dream she half-remembered. She spent the evening on the couch, flipping through streaming options, her laptop open on the coffee table. The warm glow of the living room lamp pushed the memory of the strange call further from her mind.

At 11:47 PM, as she was scrolling through her emails, her phone buzzed again.

She glanced at the screen. Unknown Number.

Her stomach tightened. She hesitated before picking it up, her finger hovering over the answer button. After a few seconds, the ringing stopped. She let out a breath she hadn't realized she'd been holding and set the phone back down. But almost immediately, it buzzed again.

This time, she answered. "Who is this?" she snapped, her voice laced with irritation.

There was silence at first, followed by that same faint crackle of static. Then, the voice returned, distorted and haunting.

"Rachel… you didn't listen."

Her blood turned cold. "Listen to what? What are you talking about?"

But the line went dead again. She stared at the phone, her hands trembling. The silence in her apartment was oppressive now, the hum of the refrigerator and the faint ticking of the wall clock only amplifying her sense of isolation.

She locked her doors and windows before retreating to her bedroom. The phone sat on her nightstand like a taunting presence. She stared at it, willing it not to ring again.

It didn't.

—-

The next day, Rachel decided to take action. She called her phone provider, asking them to trace the calls or block the number. After a frustrating back-and-forth, the representative told her the calls were coming from an unregistered source, and there was little they could do.

"Probably just a spam bot," the rep offered, trying to sound reassuring. "Happens all the time."

But Rachel wasn't reassured. She felt like she was being watched, the hairs on the back of her neck prickling whenever she turned a corner or glanced out her window.

That evening, she put her phone on silent and buried it in a drawer. She made tea, curled up with a book, and tried to distract herself. For a while, it worked. The warm tea soothed her nerves, and the soft glow of her bedside lamp made the shadows seem less menacing.

Until the phone buzzed again.

She stared at the drawer, her heart racing. She didn't want to answer, but ignoring it felt impossible. Slowly, she opened the drawer and picked up the phone. The same untraceable number flashed on the screen. Against her better judgment, she answered.

The static was louder this time, and the voice, though still distorted, was clearer. "You didn't listen," it said again.

"Listen to what?" she shouted, her fear giving way to anger.

"What do you want?"

The voice ignored her. "It's coming," it whispered. Then, more ominously: "Don't look."

Her breath hitched. "Don't look at what?"

But the line went silent once more.

Rachel's grip on the phone tightened as she looked around her room. The shadows seemed to deepen, shifting in ways that made her doubt her eyes. The voice's warning echoed in her mind: Don't look.

—-

That night, she slept with the light on. When she finally drifted into an uneasy slumber, her dreams were plagued with indistinct shapes and muffled whispers. She woke several times, drenched in sweat, her eyes darting to the phone on her nightstand. Each time, it remained still and silent.

Until 3:03 AM.

The buzzing shattered the fragile quiet. This time, the phone's screen didn't display a number at all—just a blank space where the caller ID should have been.

Rachel's hands shook as she picked it up. "Hello?" she whispered.

The voice was waiting for her. "It's here."

A sound in the apartment made her freeze—a faint creak, as though someone had stepped on a loose floorboard. She sat up, her heart pounding in her chest.

"Who's there?" she called out, her voice trembling.

No answer.

She turned on the flashlight app on her phone and shone it around the room. Nothing. But the sound came again, this time closer—a slow, deliberate creak.

The phone crackled. "Don't look."

Rachel's breath came in short, panicked gasps. "What do you mean? Don't look at what?"

But the voice was gone, leaving only the static.

The creaking stopped, replaced by a heavy silence. Rachel sat perfectly still, her flashlight trained on the bedroom door. She felt it before she saw it—a presence, something lurking just beyond the threshold. Her instincts screamed at her to stay where she was, to follow the voice's warning.

But curiosity and terror pulled her forward. Slowly, she slid out of bed, the floor cold beneath her feet. She inched toward the door, her flashlight trembling in her hand.

The hallway was empty.

Relief flooded her for a moment, but it was short-lived. From behind her, she heard a faint whisper: "You looked."

She spun around, her flashlight sweeping across the room. For a brief moment, the beam landed on something—a shape, impossibly tall and impossibly thin, standing in the corner of her bedroom. Its eyes—or where its eyes should have been—glinted faintly in the light.

The phone slipped from her hand, clattering to the floor. The light went out, plunging the room into darkness. And in the silence that followed, all Rachel could hear was her own ragged breathing—and the faint sound of static growing louder.

8

The Dying Words

The hospital room smelled of antiseptic and despair. Pale, sterile walls reflected the harsh fluorescent light overhead, and the rhythmic beep of the heart monitor was the only sound punctuating the silence. Jessica sat stiffly in the vinyl chair by the bed, her hands clutching each other so tightly her knuckles were white. She didn't belong here—not in this room, not in this moment. But here she was, summoned by a desperate call from a nurse: "Your uncle doesn't have much time. He's asking for you."

Her uncle, Robert, was the last person Jessica had expected to hear from. Estranged for years, he had drifted out of the family's lives after a scandal no one liked to discuss. Growing up, Jessica had only heard whispers about Robert's mysterious business dealings, the trouble he'd gotten into, and the debts that had seemingly swallowed him whole. He had vanished one day, leaving behind a trail of rumors and broken ties. And now, out of nowhere, he was dying—and he wanted to see her.

She shifted uncomfortably in her chair, her eyes fixed on the frail figure in the bed. Robert's once-broad shoulders were sunken, his skin pale and waxy, stretched tightly over his cheekbones. His breathing was shallow, rattling in his chest like dry leaves. He hadn't stirred since she arrived, and the nurse had warned her that he might not wake again. Still, Jessica sat and waited, unsure what to say if he did.

The minutes dragged on, and the rhythmic beeping of the monitor began to lull her into a haze of fatigue. She was just about to give up and leave when Robert's eyelids fluttered.

"Uncle Robert?" she said softly, leaning forward.

His eyes opened, glassy and unfocused at first. But then they locked onto hers with startling clarity. His lips moved, but no sound came out.

Jessica rose from her chair, leaning in closer. "I'm here," she said, her voice shaking. "It's Jessica."

He struggled to lift a hand, his fingers trembling as if the effort was almost too much. Jessica reached out and took it, startled by how cold and fragile it felt. His lips moved again, and this time, she caught the faintest whisper of words.

"Not... safe," he rasped, his voice barely audible.

Jessica frowned. "What's not safe? What do you mean?"

Robert's grip on her hand tightened with surprising strength.

His eyes were wide now, filled with a mixture of fear and urgency. "They... coming," he said, his voice cracking.

Her stomach churned. "Who's coming? Uncle Robert, I don't understand."

He coughed violently, his whole body convulsing with the effort. For a moment, Jessica thought he wouldn't recover, but then he fixed her with one last, piercing look. "The safe..." he wheezed. "Under... the clock..."

Jessica's heart raced. "What safe? What's under the clock?"

But his gaze turned glassy, his hand falling limp in hers. The heart monitor let out a long, piercing tone, and a moment later, a nurse rushed into the room. Jessica stumbled back, her mind spinning as the nurse tried in vain to revive him.

— -

The funeral was a muted affair. Only a handful of people attended, mostly distant relatives who barely knew Robert. Jessica stood apart from the small crowd, the cryptic words he had spoken to her replaying in her mind. Not safe... They're coming... The safe under the clock.

She couldn't shake the feeling that his death had left something unfinished—something he had desperately tried to tell her. And then there was the matter of his home, a crumbling old house on the outskirts of town that no one had visited in years. It was the only thing he had left behind, and as his closest living relative, it now belonged to her.

The house was exactly as she remembered it from childhood—dark, foreboding, and cloaked in an air of neglect. The windows were grimy, and the front porch sagged under the weight of years of disrepair. Jessica stood at the threshold, the key trembling in her hand. She had no idea what she was looking for, but Robert's final words echoed in her ears, urging her forward.

Inside, the air was stale and heavy, carrying the scent of dust and decay. The grandfather clock stood in the corner of the living room, just as she remembered it. Its hands were frozen at 3:15, and its once-polished wood was dull and cracked. Jessica approached it cautiously, her eyes scanning for any sign of a hidden compartment or safe.

She ran her hands along the base of the clock, her fingers searching for seams or irregularities. At first, she found nothing, but then her fingers brushed against a small, barely visible notch. Her pulse quickened as she pressed it, and with a soft click, a hidden panel slid open, revealing a small, rusted safe embedded in the wall.

Jessica stared at it, her heart pounding. She had no idea what might be inside—or if she even wanted to know. But Robert's dying words pushed her forward. She found the combination scratched onto the inside of the clock's door and entered it with trembling fingers. The safe creaked open.

Inside was a single item: a leather-bound journal. Its cover was cracked and worn, and its pages were yellowed with age. Jessica picked it up, her hands shaking. The first few pages were filled with Robert's cramped handwriting, detailing his business dealings and the debts that had driven him into hiding. But as she read further, the entries grew darker.

He wrote about men who had followed him, shadows that lingered at the edges of his vision. He described strange occurrences—doors opening and closing on their own, whispers in the dead of night, and a sense of being watched. One entry caught her attention:

"They know about the safe. They won't stop until they find it. I can't run anymore. If you're reading this, Jessica, I'm sorry. I didn't mean to drag you into this."

The final entry was scrawled in frantic, uneven lines: "They're here. God help me."

A chill ran down her spine. She closed the journal, her mind racing. Who were "they"? And what had Robert done to provoke them?

As she sat there, trying to make sense of it all, she heard it—a faint creak from the hallway. Her breath caught. The house had been silent when she arrived, but now, the air felt charged with something she couldn't explain.

"Hello?" she called out, her voice trembling.

There was no answer, but the creaking continued, slow and

deliberate, growing louder. Jessica clutched the journal to her chest and rose to her feet, her eyes darting to the shadows gathering in the corners of the room.

The creaking stopped, replaced by a faint, almost imperceptible whisper. It was coming from the direction of the grandfather clock. Jessica turned slowly, her heart hammering in her chest.

The clock's hands, frozen at 3:15 for as long as she could remember, were now moving backward. The faint whisper grew louder, filling the room with an unnatural sound that made her skin crawl.

Suddenly, the clock struck three loud chimes, and the room plunged into silence.

Jessica didn't wait to see what would happen next. She grabbed the journal and ran, her footsteps echoing through the empty house. As she reached the front door, she heard it—the sound of footsteps, heavy and deliberate, following her.

She didn't look back.

9

The Unseen Neighbor

The day Emily moved into 12 Oakwood Lane, the house across the street stood like a dark, brooding sentinel. The lawn was overgrown with yellowed grass and dandelions, its shutters hung askew, and the faint scent of mildew seemed to linger in the air. But it wasn't the dilapidated appearance of the house that unnerved her—it was its silence.

In the week she spent unpacking, Emily never saw anyone enter or leave the house. No lights ever flicked on in the evenings, no mail appeared in the old rusted box, and no movement stirred behind the tattered curtains. She had assumed the property was abandoned, yet at night, she often felt the unmistakable sensation of being watched, a prickling on the back of her neck that made her check the windows and draw the blinds tight.

One rainy evening, as she was setting up her bookshelves in the living room, a soft knock came at her door. She froze, the sound unnerving in the otherwise silent house. It wasn't a hard, deliberate knock—more like a hesitant tap, as though whoever was there was unsure if they wanted to be noticed.

Emily approached the door, her bare feet sinking into the plush rug. She peered through the peephole. Rain streaked down the glass, distorting the view, but no one was there.

Her hand hovered over the doorknob. She hesitated, then unlocked it and opened the door a crack. The street was empty, the rain drumming softly on the asphalt. She stepped out onto the porch, squinting into the dim light. That's when she noticed it—a single, sodden envelope lying on the welcome mat.

It was addressed to her in neat, precise handwriting she didn't recognize. Frowning, she picked it up and returned inside, locking the door behind her. She slid a finger under the flap and pulled out a single sheet of paper. The message was simple:

"Stay away from the house across the street."

Her stomach churned. She read the note again, her heart beating faster with every word. Who had left this? Why? And why was the house across the street any of her concern?

She peeked through the blinds, staring at the darkened windows across the way. The house loomed in the rain like a sleeping beast. For a moment, she thought she saw a flicker of move-ment behind one of the curtains—but when she blinked, it was gone.

—-

The next day, Emily couldn't shake the unease that had settled in her chest. She debated calling someone—a friend, the police—but what would she even say? That she'd received a cryptic note about an old house? They'd laugh her off.

Instead, she decided to find out more about the house herself. She spent the afternoon combing through public records online. What she found left her more confused than ever. The house had belonged to the Sanderson family for decades, but after a series of unexplained incidents—complaints of noises, sightings of figures in the windows, and even a mysterious disappearance— it had been sold to an unnamed buyer. The records stopped there.

Emily leaned back in her chair, chewing her lip. The lack of information only fueled her curiosity. If someone lived there now, why were they so secretive? And if no one lived there, why did it feel like someone—or something—was watching her?

—-

That night, she woke to the sound of shattering glass. Her eyes flew open, and for a moment, she lay frozen in bed, her ears straining.

The noise had come from downstairs.

Heart pounding, she grabbed her phone and crept out of bed, her feet making no sound on the carpet. As she descended the stairs, the faint glow of the streetlamp outside spilled through the front window, casting long, eerie shadows across the living room.

The source of the noise was immediately clear—a small rock lay on the floor near the window, surrounded by shards of broken glass. Someone had thrown it hard enough to crack the thick pane. She picked up the rock, her hand shaking, and noticed another piece of paper tied around it with twine.

She unfolded it and read:
   "I warned you. Stop looking."

Emily's breath hitched. Her gaze darted to the darkened house across the street. For the first time since she moved in, one of its windows was lit, a dim, flickering glow that seemed to pulse like a heartbeat. She felt her blood run cold.

—-

Against her better judgment, Emily decided she couldn't let the strange warnings go unanswered. The next day, just as dusk settled over the neighborhood, she crossed the street and stood in front of the mysterious house. Its warped wooden door loomed before her, the paint peeling like dead skin. She raised a trembling fist and knocked.

The sound echoed, hollow and empty. She waited. No answer.

She knocked again, louder this time, but the house remained silent. Swallowing her fear, she reached for the doorknob. To her surprise, it turned easily, and the door creaked open on rusted hinges.

The smell hit her first—damp, musty air mixed with something sour and metallic. The interior was shrouded in darkness, but as her eyes adjusted, she could make out the outlines of furniture covered in white sheets, like forgotten ghosts.

"Hello?" she called out, her voice barely above a whisper.

The only response was the sound of her own breathing.

She stepped inside, her shoes crunching on something brittle. Looking down, she saw shards of broken glass scattered across the floor. Her pulse quickened as she realized the glass had fallen inward, not outward. Someone had been watching from inside.

As she moved further into the house, a faint noise caught her attention—a rhythmic creaking, like the sound of a rocking chair. Her steps faltered. The noise was coming from upstairs.

Against every instinct screaming at her to leave, she climbed the staircase. The creaking grew louder with each step. When she reached the top, she saw the door to a room at the end of the hall was ajar, a soft light spilling out.

She approached slowly, her heart hammering. She pushed the door open and froze.

The room was empty except for a single rocking chair, which swayed back and forth of its own accord. A dim lamp sat on a table nearby, casting long shadows across the walls. And in the chair, placed carefully on the seat, was a mirror.

Emily stepped closer, her reflection staring back at her. But something was wrong. Her reflection was smiling.

She wasn't.

The realization hit her like a punch to the gut. She stumbled back, her hands trembling. The mirror's surface rippled like water, and her reflection leaned forward, its grin widening.

"They told you not to look," it whispered.

The lamp flickered, and the room plunged into darkness. Emily spun around, her breath coming in short, panicked gasps. The door slammed shut behind her, and she heard it—the faint sound of footsteps circling the room, though she couldn't see a thing.

A low, guttural laugh echoed in the darkness.

She didn't remember running out of the house. Her next clear thought was standing on her front porch, gasping for air, her hands clutching the railing for support. Across the street, the house was dark again, silent and brooding as if nothing had happened.

But Emily knew better now. The house wasn't empty. And whoever—or whatever—lived there didn't want her to leave.

10

The Clock Ticking

The first time Olivia noticed the clock, it was an unremarkable Wednesday afternoon. She'd been scrolling through her emails, ignoring the growing pile of paperwork on her desk, when her phone buzzed. It wasn't the usual chirp of a notification or a text—it was a low, droning vibration that seemed to linger, resonating in her bones.

When she glanced at the screen, her brow furrowed. The display showed no name or number, just a single message:

"00:72:48."

At first, Olivia dismissed it as spam or some kind of prank. She locked her phone and tossed it back onto the desk, focusing instead on her overdue reports. But the unease lingered, like an itch at the back of her mind. Seventy-two minutes and forty-eight seconds... It didn't make sense. The number didn't match a time, a date, or any format she recognized.

By the time she left the office that evening, she'd nearly forgotten about the message. But as she climbed into her car and set her phone in the holder, the screen lit up again. The same sequence, only now the numbers were different:

"00:36:12."

Her stomach dropped. The realization was immediate and chilling. It was a countdown.

—-

Driving home, Olivia couldn't shake the growing sense of dread. She turned on the radio to drown out her thoughts, but the words of the DJ seemed distant, muted under the hum of her anxiety. She glanced at her phone more times than she cared to admit, each look confirming what she already knew: the numbers were ticking down, second by second.

By the time she pulled into her driveway, the countdown was at "00:19:03."

She stared at the glowing numbers, her hands gripping the steering wheel so tightly her knuckles turned white. Who would send this? And why? Was it a threat? A warning? Her logical mind raced through possibilities—friends playing a joke, a weird app glitch—but none of them felt right.

Finally, she grabbed her phone and stepped into her house, locking the door behind her. She had less than twenty minutes. She decided to call someone—anyone—who might make sense of the situation.

Her fingers hovered over her best friend's contact, but before she could dial, the phone buzzed in her hand. Another message appeared, stark and chilling:

"Don't call anyone."

The words felt like ice water poured over her. Olivia's gaze darted around the room, her breath quickening. Was someone watching her? She rushed to the windows, pulling the curtains shut, her heartbeat thundering in her ears.

The countdown read "00:13:45."

— -

Panic set in. Olivia paced the living room, the glow of the phone in her hand illuminating her every step. She thought about calling the police, but the cryptic message replayed in her mind. What if whoever sent it was serious? What if making the call triggered... whatever this was?

She noticed her laptop on the coffee table and snatched it up, desperate to find answers. Her fingers flew over the keyboard as she typed variations of her situation into search engines: "countdown text message," "anonymous clock countdown," "phone hacking threats." Each search returned irrelevant results—scams, conspiracy theories, urban legends.

But one thread on a shadowy forum caught her attention. The

title read:

"If you receive the countdown, DO NOT ignore it."

Her eyes scanned the post, her pulse quickening with every word. It described an eerie phenomenon—people receiving unexplained countdowns, each tied to a mysterious event. Some claimed it was a warning of imminent danger; others believed it was a twisted psychological experiment. The stories varied, but one detail remained constant: when the timer hit zero, something always happened.

Her phone buzzed again. Another message:

"12 minutes. Go to your basement."

Olivia froze. She didn't have a basement.

Shaking, she typed back a response, her fingers trembling:

"Who is this? What do you want?"

The reply came instantly:

"Go to the basement. Now."

—-

Her heart racing, Olivia searched her house. Every corner, every crevice. No basement. No hidden door. Nothing. She was certain of it. She collapsed onto the floor, her back pressed against the wall, her eyes locked on the dwindling timer: "00:07:53."

The urge to run consumed her. If this was a threat, she needed to leave, get somewhere public, call the police despite the warnings. She grabbed her keys and bolted for the front door. But as she reached for the handle, her phone buzzed again. She looked down, her breath catching in her throat.

"If you leave, it won't stop."

Her hand fell away from the door. Tears welled in her eyes, frustration mingling with fear. "What do you want from me?" she whispered into the empty house.

The clock now read "00:05:22."

—-

It was then she heard it—a faint scraping sound, like nails dragging across wood. It came from beneath her. The floor.

Olivia's blood ran cold. She crouched down, pressing her ear to the floorboards. The sound grew louder, rhythmic, deliberate.

She scrambled back, staring at the wooden planks as though they might burst open at any moment. Her mind raced. Had she missed something? A trapdoor? An old access point? She tried to remember the blueprints from when she'd bought the house, but nothing came to mind.

Another buzz. Another message:
  "Look closer."

Against every instinct, she crawled forward and began knocking on the floorboards. The third one she tapped sounded hollow. Her heart lurched. Grabbing a nearby screwdriver, she pried it loose.

What she found beneath wasn't a basement, but a narrow tunnel, descending into darkness.

The timer read "00:03:14."

— -

Adrenaline took over. Gripping her phone tightly, she lowered herself into the tunnel. The air was damp and cold, the smell of earth and decay overwhelming. The narrow walls pressed against her shoulders as she descended, the dim light from her phone barely illuminating the path ahead.

The scraping noise grew louder, closer. It wasn't coming from below—it was coming from behind her. She whipped around, her phone's light slicing through the dark, but saw nothing. Her breathing came in shallow gasps as she quickened her pace.

The tunnel opened into a small, dimly lit chamber. In the center sat an old grandfather clock, its brass pendulum swinging steadily. The sight of it sent a wave of dread crashing over her. The clock was ancient, its face weathered and cracked, but the hands moved in perfect synchronization with the countdown on her phone.

"00:01:27."

Another message appeared:
"Stop the clock."

Olivia hesitated. The pendulum's motion was hypnotic, almost soothing, yet every fiber of her being screamed that this clock was wrong, unnatural. Her hands shook as she reached for the pendulum. The moment her fingers brushed it, the chamber filled with a deafening screech, like metal tearing against metal. She clapped her hands over her ears, dropping the phone.

The countdown on the screen flashed red:
"00:00:32."

— -

Desperation overtook her. She grabbed the clock's hands and twisted them backward, but they resisted, as though some unseen force held them in place. The screeching intensified, the walls of the chamber trembling. Dust rained from above, and the air grew thicker, harder to breathe.

"00:00:10."

She screamed, pounding on the clock, yanking at the pendulum, clawing at its face. It wouldn't budge.

"00:00:05."

Tears streamed down her face as she gave one final, desperate pull. The pendulum snapped free, and the clock's hands froze at zero.

The noise stopped.

The chamber was silent, save for Olivia's ragged breathing. She stared at the motionless clock, her body trembling. Relief began to wash over her—until she saw her phone.

It wasn't blank. A new countdown had begun.

This time, it was longer.

"72:00:00."

And below it, a single word:
  "Next."

11

The Dead Call

The first call came at 11:03 p.m. Leah was seated on the couch, the soft glow of her reading lamp casting shadows across the room. A half-empty mug of tea sat on the coffee table, its steam curling lazily in the still air. She was deep into a novel, its suspenseful plot gripping her attention, when her phone buzzed on the side table.

She glanced at the screen. No Caller ID.

Leah frowned. She wasn't in the mood for telemarketers or scams. Without answering, she silenced the phone and set it face down. But before she could return to her book, it buzzed again.

No Caller ID.

The second time gave her pause. She stared at the screen, unease creeping into her chest. Reluctantly, she picked it up and swiped to answer.

"Hello?" she said, her voice tentative.

There was silence on the other end. Not the static-filled background of a dropped call, but a complete, suffocating void. Leah held her breath, waiting. Just as she was about to hang up, a voice emerged from the darkness, faint but unmistakable.

"Leah..."

She froze. Her heart pounded in her chest, her grip on the phone tightening. It wasn't just any voice. It was her mother's.

Her mother, who had died three years ago.

—-

"Who—who is this?" Leah stammered, her voice trembling.

The line crackled, the faint sound of static whispering in her ear. Then the voice came again, soft and mournful. "Leah... I need you to listen."

Tears welled in her eyes as her throat constricted. "This isn't funny. Who are you?" she demanded, her voice breaking. But deep down, she knew. The inflection, the tone, even the slight lilt of the vowels—it was her mother. It couldn't be, but it was.

"I don't have much time," the voice continued. "You need to leave the house. Now."

The line went dead.

Leah stared at the phone, her hands shaking. Her rational mind screamed that it was a cruel prank, a sick joke someone had orchestrated to unsettle her. But the part of her still grieving, still aching from her mother's loss, couldn't dismiss the familiarity of the voice.

She placed the phone on the coffee table, her breathing uneven. Her home was quiet, the only sound the ticking of the clock on the wall. For several minutes, she sat motionless, staring at the phone as though it might come to life again.

When it buzzed a third time, she nearly screamed.

— -

The screen flashed No Caller ID once more. She hesitated, her thumb hovering over the answer button. Finally, she slid her finger across the screen.

"Hello?" she whispered.

This time, the voice was louder, more urgent. "Leah, you have to go. They're coming."

Her stomach churned. "Who's coming?" she asked, her voice barely audible. But instead of an answer, there was a sound—faint at first, then growing louder. It was a rhythmic tapping, like fingers drumming on a hard surface.

Her head whipped around, scanning the room. The noise wasn't coming from the phone. It was coming from the front door.

— -

Leah's body stiffened, her muscles locked in place as fear coursed through her veins. She stared at the door, her mind racing. It was late—too late for visitors—and she hadn't heard anyone approach. The tapping continued, steady and deliberate.

She rose from the couch, moving as silently as possible. The phone remained clutched in her hand, its screen still glowing. She crept toward the door, her pulse thundering in her ears. Through the peephole, she could see nothing but darkness.

"Who's there?" she called, her voice trembling.

The tapping stopped. For a moment, there was nothing but silence, thick and oppressive. Then a voice spoke, low and gravelly.

"We're here for you, Leah."

She stumbled back, her breath hitching. The voice wasn't familiar. It was cold, devoid of emotion, and it sent chills racing down her spine.

The phone buzzed again. She glanced at the screen. This time, instead of No Caller ID, the name displayed sent her reeling: Mom.

— -

Her legs threatened to give out beneath her. It wasn't possible—her mother's phone number had been deactivated after her death. Hands shaking, she answered the call.

"Mom?" she whispered, her voice breaking.

"Leah, listen to me," her mother's voice said urgently. "You're in danger. They're inside."

Leah's heart stopped. She spun around, her eyes darting across the room. Nothing seemed out of place, but the shadows in the corners suddenly felt deeper, more menacing. The air was heavy, as though the walls were pressing inward.

Her mother's voice continued, frantic now. "The back door. Go."

Leah didn't wait to question it. She sprinted toward the kitchen, her bare feet slapping against the cold tiles. As she reached the back door, she fumbled with the lock, her hands slick with sweat. Finally, it clicked open, and she threw the door wide.

The night air hit her like a slap, cold and biting. She stumbled out onto the porch, gasping for breath. Behind her, the house loomed, its windows dark and unwelcoming. She glanced back, expecting to see someone—something—emerging from the shadows. But the doorway was empty.

Her phone buzzed again. She stared at the screen, tears blurring her vision.

"Don't stop running."

—-

Leah bolted into the yard, her legs pumping beneath her. The world was eerily silent, the only sound her ragged breaths and the crunch of leaves underfoot. She didn't know where she was going—only that she had to get as far from the house as possible.

She reached the edge of the property, where the trees loomed tall and imposing. The forest was dense, the darkness impenetrable. Her phone buzzed once more, and she hesitated, glancing at the screen.

"They're close."

Behind her, she heard it: the sound of footsteps, deliberate and heavy. She turned, her eyes searching the shadows, but there was nothing. No movement, no figure—only the sense of something watching her, waiting.

"Leah..."

The whisper came from everywhere and nowhere, wrapping around her like a suffocating shroud. She spun around, her phone's weak light cutting through the darkness, but the beam revealed only empty space.

"Mom?" she called, her voice trembling.

The footsteps grew louder, closer. She couldn't see them, but she felt them—an oppressive presence bearing down on her.

She turned and ran.

— -

The forest closed in around her, the branches clawing at her skin. Her lungs burned, her legs aching with every step. The phone buzzed incessantly in her hand, but she didn't dare stop to look.

Finally, she broke into a clearing, collapsing onto the ground. She gasped for air, her chest heaving as she glanced back at the path she'd taken. The forest was silent again, the footsteps gone.

Her phone buzzed one last time. She raised it to her face, the screen glowing with a single message:

"You can't escape them."

The voice came from behind her, low and cold. "We never left, Leah."

Before she could scream, the world went black.

12

The Reflection

Rain pattered against the bathroom window, a steady rhythm that filled the silence of the house. Evie stood in front of the mirror, her hands gripping the edge of the sink. The fluorescent light above flickered faintly, casting a pale, inconsistent glow on the tiled walls. Her reflection stared back at her, weary and hollow-eyed.

It had been another sleepless night. Dark circles rimmed her eyes, and her skin looked sallow, almost translucent under the harsh light. She had barely eaten in days. Every sound, every flicker of movement in the corner of her vision made her heart race. But this—this was something else.

She leaned closer to the mirror, studying her reflection. At first, she thought her mind was playing tricks on her, a product of her exhaustion. But no matter how long she stared, it didn't go away.

Her reflection was... wrong.

—-

Evie turned her head to the right, and her reflection followed—but not quite in sync. The movement was a fraction of a second too slow, like a lagging video feed. She raised her hand, and again, her reflection mirrored her, but with the same disjointed delay.

Her breath quickened, fogging the glass in front of her. She stepped back, blinking hard as if to clear her vision. "It's just the light," she muttered under her breath. "I'm tired. I'm seeing things."

She flicked the light switch off and then on again, hoping the sudden brightness would banish the unease clawing at her chest. But when her gaze returned to the mirror, her reflection hadn't moved. It was still standing as it had been before she flicked the switch, staring straight at her.

A jolt of cold fear shot through her. She stumbled backward, her heel catching on the edge of the rug, and she fell hard against the wall. Her reflection moved now, but the motion wasn't hers—it was deliberate, slow, and unsettling.

"Who—what—" Evie's voice cracked. She couldn't tear her eyes away from the mirror. Her reflection tilted its head, a crooked smile creeping across its face. A smile she wasn't making.

—-

The silence in the room was suffocating. Even the rain outside seemed to have ceased, as if the world were holding its breath. Evie scrambled to her feet, her legs trembling. "This isn't real," she whispered, backing away from the sink. "It's not real."

Her reflection raised a hand and placed it flat against the other side of the glass, the motion so slow it was almost taunting. Evie froze, her heart hammering in her chest. She could see every detail of the hand pressed against the mirror—the faint lines on the palm, the chipped nail polish on the fingers. It was hers, and yet it wasn't.

"You can't leave."

The voice was low and echoing, as though it were coming from deep within the glass itself. It wasn't her voice, but it carried the same cadence, the same timbre. It was hers but twisted, corrupted.

Evie screamed, grabbing a towel from the nearby rack and throwing it over the mirror. The fabric hung there, covering the glass, and for a moment, the room was still. She took a deep breath, her hands clutching the counter for support.

But then, beneath the towel, she saw movement. The outline of a hand pressed against the fabric, its fingers curling and dragging downward as though trying to claw its way out.

—-

Evie bolted from the bathroom, slamming the door shut behind her. She leaned against it, her chest heaving as she tried to catch her breath. Her phone was on the kitchen counter—she could call someone, anyone, for help. She just needed to calm down, think rationally.

The hallway stretched before her, dimly lit by a single bulb. Shadows danced along the walls as the light flickered. She hesitated, glancing over her shoulder at the closed bathroom door. Nothing moved, no sounds came from within.

Summoning her courage, she edged toward the kitchen. Each step felt heavier than the last, the air thick and oppressive. When she finally reached her phone, she snatched it up, her fingers trembling as she dialed her best friend, Alyssa.

The call went straight to voicemail.

"Damn it," Evie muttered. She tried again, and again, the result was the same. Frustrated, she opened her messages and typed out a quick text.

"Something's wrong. Call me as soon as you get this."

She hit send and set the phone down, pacing the kitchen. Her thoughts raced, each one more frantic than the last. She couldn't go back into the bathroom—not yet—but she couldn't ignore what she'd seen either.

The sound of her phone buzzing on the counter made her jump. She snatched it up, relief flooding her as she saw Alyssa's name on the screen.

"Alyssa! Thank God," she said, her voice shaky.

But the voice on the other end wasn't Alyssa's.

"You shouldn't have left."

——

Evie's blood ran cold. The voice was the same one from the mirror, distorted and chilling. She dropped the phone as though it had burned her, the screen shattering on the tiled floor. The voice continued, now coming from the broken device.

"You can't escape me, Evie."

The words echoed through the room, impossibly loud. Evie clamped her hands over her ears, backing away until her back hit the refrigerator. "Leave me alone!" she screamed.

The voice laughed, a sound that made her skin crawl. "I am you, Evie. You can't run from yourself."

Suddenly, every reflective surface in the room came alive. The glass on the oven door, the stainless steel of the fridge, even the black screen of the TV in the adjacent living room—they all displayed her reflection. Each one moved independently, some smiling, others glaring, their eyes following her every move.

Evie's breath hitched as the reflections began to speak in unison. "Come back to me, Evie. Come back to where you belong."

—-

She bolted from the kitchen, her feet pounding against the floor as she ran to her bedroom. Slamming the door shut, she pushed a dresser in front of it, barricading herself inside. Her hands trembled as she grabbed a lamp and yanked the cord from the wall, plunging the room into darkness.

In the pitch black, she felt momentarily safe. No reflections. No mirrors. Just darkness.

But then she heard it—a soft tapping on the vanity mirror across the room.

"Let me in," the voice whispered, so close it felt like it was inside her head.

Evie huddled in the corner, clutching the lamp like a weapon. Tears streamed down her face as she whispered to herself, "It's not real. It's not real."

The tapping grew louder, more insistent. Suddenly, the mirror cracked, spiderwebbing from the center outward. Through the fractured glass, she saw her reflection staring back at her, its face twisted into a grotesque grin.

"You can't hide forever," it said, reaching out through the shards.

Evie screamed as the glass shattered completely, the pieces flying toward her like razor-sharp confetti. She shielded her face, the shards cutting into her arms and legs. When the chaos subsided, she dared to look up.

The mirror was gone. So was the reflection.

But in the silence that followed, a single whisper echoed through the room.

"I'll always be here."

13

The Last Train

The station was eerily quiet, its usual bustle replaced by an unsettling stillness. Amelia clutched her coat tighter around her, the cold night air biting through the fabric as she scanned the dimly lit platform. A single flickering bulb buzzed overhead, casting sporadic shadows that danced along the cracked concrete.

The announcement crackled over the intercom, the voice distorted but clear enough to make her stomach sink.

"Last train arriving in three minutes. All passengers, please proceed to the platform."

Amelia glanced around. She was the only passenger. It wasn't unusual for this time of night—she had caught the last train before, though never so late. Tonight, however, felt different. The silence wasn't comforting; it was oppressive, and the faint echoes of distant footsteps—unseen and inconsistent—set her nerves on edge.

The train's horn sounded faintly in the distance, a mournful wail that seemed to vibrate through the empty station. She exhaled, her breath forming pale clouds in the air, and stepped closer to the edge of the platform. The track stretched into the darkness, its steel rails glinting faintly under the weak station lights.

When the train finally emerged, its headlights cutting through the night, she felt a strange sense of relief—mixed with a gnawing unease. It slowed to a crawl, hissing and groaning as it came to a stop. The doors slid open with a metallic screech, revealing an empty car bathed in dim yellow light.

Amelia hesitated.

—-

She glanced over her shoulder, half-expecting someone else to appear on the platform. But it was still just her, the station as deserted as ever. With a small shake of her head, she stepped onto the train, her boots clunking against the metal floor.

The doors closed behind her with a loud clunk, and the train lurched forward, the momentum forcing her to grab onto a pole for balance. The silence inside the car was suffocating, broken only by the faint hum of the train's engine and the occasional squeal of the wheels on the tracks.

Amelia chose a seat near the middle of the car, sliding into the cracked vinyl. She placed her bag on her lap and pulled out her phone, hoping to distract herself until her stop. But the screen remained stubbornly dark. She pressed the power button again, harder this time, but it didn't respond.

"No signal either," she muttered, glancing at the blank bars in the corner. Typical.

The train picked up speed, the station lights outside becoming streaks of white and orange. She settled into her seat, trying to shake off the unease that clung to her like a second skin. The rhythmic clatter of the wheels was almost soothing, lulling her into a false sense of calm.

Until she noticed the man.

—-

He was sitting at the far end of the car, his head down and face obscured by the brim of a wide hat. Amelia froze, her grip tightening on her bag. She could've sworn the train was empty when she boarded—she had checked every seat.

Hadn't she?

The man didn't move, his stillness unnatural. His hands rested on his lap, gloved and motionless. Amelia's breath hitched as she tried to recall if he'd been there when she boarded, but her memory felt strangely hazy.

She debated moving to another car but dismissed the idea almost as quickly as it came. The man hadn't done anything—yet. And besides, she'd have to pass him to reach the door, an idea that made her stomach churn.

Instead, she shifted in her seat, pulling her bag closer and forcing herself to look away. She stared out the window, though there was little to see. The landscape outside was a blur of darkness, the occasional streetlight or shadowy structure flashing by too quickly to make sense of.

Minutes passed, though it felt much longer. The train swayed gently on the tracks, its motion almost hypnotic. But no announcement came for the next stop. Amelia frowned, glancing at the digital display near the ceiling. The screen was blank, save for a faint static that danced across its surface.

"Next stop, Juniper Street," she whispered to herself, trying to remember the route. Juniper was always the next station after midnight. But the train didn't slow.

The man moved.

— -

It was subtle, almost imperceptible—a slight tilt of his head. Amelia's gaze snapped back to him, her heart pounding in her chest. He hadn't moved a muscle before now, and the sudden shift made her pulse race. His face remained obscured, the brim of his hat casting a shadow that seemed deeper than it should have been.

She tried to focus on her breathing, telling herself that he was just another late-night traveler. Maybe he was just as nervous as she was. But a voice in the back of her mind whispered otherwise.

Then the lights flickered.

The train plunged into darkness for a split second, the sudden change jarring and absolute. When the lights came back on, the man was closer.

He hadn't stood. He hadn't walked. He was simply... closer, seated two rows ahead of where he had been.

Amelia's breath caught in her throat. She clutched her bag tighter, her knuckles white against the fabric. Her gaze darted to the door at the far end of the car. It was locked.

The lights flickered again.

Darkness swallowed the car, longer this time, and when the lights returned, he was closer still. One row ahead now, his gloved hands resting on his knees, his head still tilted at that unnatural angle.

"Who are you?" Amelia's voice trembled, barely above a whisper.

He didn't respond.

The train began to slow, the screech of the brakes deafening in the silence. Relief flooded her—finally, a station. She didn't care which one; she just needed to get off this train.

The doors slid open with a hiss, revealing a platform bathed in dim, flickering light. Amelia bolted from her seat, her bag clutched tightly against her chest as she rushed toward the exit.

She stepped onto the platform, her boots echoing against the concrete. But the relief was short-lived.

The station was identical to the one she had left.

—-

Her heart sank as she turned to look back at the train. The man was standing now, his figure a shadow against the yellow glow of the car. He didn't move toward her, but his presence was enough to send a shiver down her spine.

The train's horn blared, and the doors slid shut. It pulled away from the platform, disappearing into the darkness.

Amelia turned, her breath coming in ragged gasps as she scanned the station. It was empty, just like the one before. The same flickering bulb, the same cracked concrete. Even the vending machine in the corner looked identical, down to the graffiti scrawled on its side.

Panic bubbled in her chest. This wasn't possible.

She heard it then—a sound that froze her blood.

The faint echo of footsteps.

Amelia spun around, her eyes darting across the empty platform. There was no one there. The sound grew louder, closer, and yet she couldn't see its source.

"Hello?" she called out, her voice shaky.

The footsteps stopped.

For a moment, there was only silence. Then, from the shadows at the far end of the platform, a figure emerged.

It was the man.

He stepped into the dim light, his face still obscured by the brim of his hat. But this time, he raised his head.

Amelia's scream echoed through the empty station, swallowed by the endless dark.

14

The Lurking Shadow

The wind howled through the cracks in the windows, sending icy drafts swirling through the empty house. Lily tugged her blanket tighter around her shoulders, her eyes fixed on the dim hallway just beyond the living room. The clock on the mantel ticked steadily, each second dragging on like an eternity. Her pulse quickened with every passing moment. The house felt colder than usual tonight, colder than it ever had before.

It had been three months since she had moved into her grand-mother's old house, and in that time, Lily had convinced herself that she was overreacting. Yes, it was an old house, creaking and groaning as if it had a life of its own. Yes, the floorboards had a way of whispering underfoot, and the shadows seemed to stretch unnaturally along the walls, but there was nothing inherently wrong with the house. Nothing she couldn't explain. Or so she thought.

But tonight, something was different.

Lily had been sitting in the living room, reading, when she first heard the sound. A soft scrape, like the brush of a shoe against the floor. It was faint at first, so faint she thought it was just the house settling. But then it came again, louder this time, unmistakable. She set her book down, holding her breath. The sound was coming from the hallway—the same hallway that had always felt... off to her. The hallway that stretched down into the heart of the house, where the shadows were always thicker and the air always seemed colder.

She had tried to ignore it, tried to tell herself it was nothing. But the sound persisted, a slow, deliberate scrape that came at regular intervals, like footsteps.

Her pulse raced. She was alone tonight. She had been alone for hours. The idea of someone else being in the house was absurd, but the longer the sound continued, the more unsettled she became.

Lily rose slowly from the couch, her bare feet making no noise against the cold hardwood floor. She moved quietly, her heart pounding as she approached the edge of the hallway. The scraping sound was still there, but now it was accompanied by a soft shuffle, like something—or someone—was dragging something heavy across the floor. She strained her ears, trying to pinpoint the source. It was coming from the second bedroom at the end of the hall.

She hesitated, her mind racing with a dozen different possibilities. Her grandmother's old house had always felt like a place frozen in time, but that didn't mean it was completely without its quirks. The house creaked and groaned as it settled, and there were countless things she could attribute this to: a loose board, a shifting beam, maybe an old piece of furniture that had been disturbed. But the feeling in the pit of her stomach told her otherwise.

The temperature in the hallway dropped, and Lily felt a cold draft brush against her skin, sending a shiver up her spine. She reached for the light switch but stopped short when the scraping sound grew louder. It was closer now, more pronounced, as if whatever was causing it was moving down the hall toward her.

Lily's breath caught in her throat. She should leave. Should run out of the house, call the police, do something—anything—but her feet remained rooted to the spot. She couldn't bring herself to turn around and flee, not with the sound of footsteps—or whatever it was—so close behind her. The hairs on the back of her neck stood on end, and she fought to keep her breathing steady.

"Hello?" she called out, her voice barely above a whisper. The hallway stretched before her like a dark tunnel, shadows clinging to every corner. The scraping sound stopped, and for a moment, there was only silence. The silence was worse than the noise. It was suffocating.

Then, the sound came again. Closer. So close, in fact, that Lily could swear it was right behind her. She spun around, her heart leaping into her throat, but there was nothing there. No one. Just the dark hallway, the same as before. She turned back, her eyes wide, searching for anything that might explain the noise.

Nothing.

And yet, something was there. She felt it—a presence, like someone was watching her, standing just out of sight, waiting.

Lily took a hesitant step back, her eyes fixed on the darkened doorway at the end of the hall. The second bedroom. The source of the noise. She didn't know what she expected to find, but the air felt thicker there, heavier. It was as though the room itself was holding its breath.

She swallowed hard and took another step, her feet unwilling to move any faster. The scraping sound had stopped again, but the shuffling noise remained. It was like the sound of something— or someone—slowly dragging their feet across the floor. Slowly and deliberately.

Her pulse quickened.

With trembling fingers, Lily reached for the door handle. The metal was cold under her touch, the handle slick with sweat. She could feel her heart pounding in her chest as she turned the handle, pushing the door open just a crack.

The room was pitch black. The only light was the faint glow from the hallway behind her, casting long, distorted shadows on the walls. For a moment, she stood there, holding her breath, unsure if she should step inside. Then, as if in response to her hesitation, the shuffling sound started again, louder now, coming from the far side of the room.

She jumped back, but the door was already open, and her curiosity, however foolish, got the better of her. She pushed it the rest of the way open and stepped inside, her heart racing.

The room was cold. Cold in a way that didn't make sense, even for a house this old. It felt like the temperature had dropped several degrees in just a few seconds, and Lily shivered involuntarily. She could barely make out the outlines of the furniture in the dark, but it didn't matter. There was something in the corner of the room, just beyond her line of sight. She could hear it now, the unmistakable sound of something—or someone—moving.

The shuffling noise came closer, and Lily's breath caught in her throat. She had no idea what was making the sound, but she knew one thing for certain: it wasn't just the house settling.

Something—or someone—was in the room with her.

The door slammed shut behind her with a deafening crash, and Lily whipped around in panic. The coldness in the room intensified, making her teeth chatter. The shuffling stopped. The silence was unbearable.

Then, the shadow moved.

At first, it was just a flicker at the edge of her vision, but it quickly grew larger, more distinct, as though something—or someone—was creeping toward her from the corner of the room. She couldn't see a face, no details, just a shifting shadow that seemed to stretch out from the darkness, closing in on her.

Her breath came in ragged gasps as she backed toward the door, her hand groping blindly for the handle. But the door wouldn't open. The knob twisted uselessly in her hand, the cold metal slick and unyielding.

The shadow loomed closer, its shape indistinct but undeniably there. Lily's pulse thundered in her ears as the darkness around her deepened, suffocating her.

With a final, desperate scream, she yanked at the door again, her fingers raw with the effort. And just as the shadow reached her, the door creaked open.

She stumbled backward into the hallway, gasping for air, her body trembling. The door slammed shut behind her, and the shadow was gone.

But the house—quiet, still—was not. The presence that had been lurking in the room had followed her into the hall. It was still there, watching, waiting for her to make the next move.

<h1 style="text-align:center">15</h1>

The Unopened Box

The rain beat against the windows with relentless intensity, like a thousand tiny hammers striking the glass in time with the thunder. Lily sat in the living room, her back pressed into the worn armchair, her eyes fixed on the small, nondescript box that sat on the coffee table in front of her. It had been there for two days now, unopened, its plain brown surface devoid of any identifying marks. There was no return address, no note, nothing to indicate who had sent it—or why.

Lily had been hesitant to open it. The moment it arrived, something in her gut told her to leave it alone. But now, after two days of constant staring, of wondering what lay inside, the curiosity gnawed at her. The house was silent, except for the tapping of the rain and the occasional rumble of distant thunder. It was as if the storm itself had wrapped the world in an eerie cocoon, making the house feel even more isolated, as though she were the last person on Earth.

Her fingers twitched as she reached for the box. It was small, only about the size of a shoe box, and surprisingly heavy for its size. She turned it over in her hands, hoping for some clue—some indication of its contents—but there was nothing. Just that dull, unremarkable surface.

Lily's breath quickened as she pried open the flap of the box. The cardboard groaned in protest, as if resisting her touch. Inside, there was only one object. A small, intricately carved wooden box, no bigger than a jewelry case, nestled within the larger box like it was a treasure meant to be hidden away. It was smooth and polished, its surface dark and gleaming under the dim light. The wood seemed to shimmer, the intricate patterns carved into it catching the faint light from the lamp nearby.

Lily's hand trembled slightly as she reached for the smaller box. She could feel a chill in the air, though the room was warm enough. Her fingers brushed the surface of the box, and for a moment, she thought she felt something like a pulse—something alive under the wood. She quickly pulled her hand back, shaking her head. Ridiculous. It was just a box, right? Just an innocent object. There was nothing strange about it.

But then why did it feel like the air around her had shifted?

Taking a deep breath, Lily set the small wooden box down on the coffee table and inspected it more closely. The carvings on the lid were delicate, almost hypnotic, swirling around in an elegant design. She couldn't quite make out what the images depicted—figures, shapes, symbols, maybe—but they seemed... familiar, somehow. Her mind struggled to make sense of them, but they kept slipping away, as though they were teasing her from the edges of her memory.

Her fingers hovered over the lid of the box. There was no lock, no clasp, just a smooth, unbroken surface. Tentatively, she lifted the lid.

Inside the box was a small bundle wrapped in faded cloth. It looked like some kind of fabric—dark and weathered, with frayed edges where it had been hastily tied. Lily hesitated. Her heart raced in her chest, and a prickling sensation crawled across her skin. What was inside that bundle? Why had someone gone to such lengths to send it to her?

She untied the cloth carefully, unfolding it in stages, revealing a small object wrapped inside. As the last corner of fabric fell away, Lily gasped.

It was a ring.

The ring was simple, made of tarnished silver, with a thin band that seemed to have been shaped by hand. But it was the stone set in the center that caught her attention. It was black, but not just black—deep, inky black, with an almost unnatural sheen to it. The stone seemed to shift in the light, its surface reflecting the room in strange ways. It was like looking into the void, as if the stone had no end, no beginning, just an endless depth that threatened to pull her in.

Lily stared at it, her fingers frozen in place. She felt drawn to it in a way that she couldn't explain, an almost magnetic pull that made her breath catch in her throat. The air in the room felt thick now, heavy, as if something had changed. She shook her head, trying to clear her thoughts, but the feeling persisted.

The sound of the wind outside seemed to pick up, rattling the windows with sudden force, and the house groaned in response, its old bones creaking like they were shifting under the weight of the storm. Lily felt a sudden surge of unease. There was something about the ring—something she couldn't shake. It was too still, too quiet. As if it had been waiting for her. Waiting for her to open the box.

She couldn't resist any longer. Her fingers closed around the ring, and she lifted it from its cloth. The stone seemed to pulse in her hand, and for a brief moment, she swore she heard a faint whisper, just at the edge of her hearing. It was like a voice, too soft to be real, a voice that seemed to come from deep within the ring itself.

Her heart raced, and she dropped the ring back into the box with a jolt, her fingers trembling. She stood up quickly, her pulse hammering in her ears. There was a strange coldness in the room now, a heaviness in the air that made her stomach churn. She needed to get rid of it. Throw it away. Burn it. Whatever it took to get rid of that feeling.

But something held her back.

She wanted to open it again. She needed to know more about it. There was a part of her, a dangerous, insistent part, that couldn't stop thinking about the ring. She glanced at it again, lying there in the box. The way it seemed to draw her in, calling to her like something ancient and forgotten. She knew she shouldn't, but she couldn't resist.

The wind howled louder now, the rain pounding harder against the windows, the storm raging outside in a frenzy. The air in the room felt charged, like the very walls were alive, closing in around her.

With a shaking hand, Lily reached for the box again. She opened it slowly, and this time, as she lifted the ring from its resting place, she didn't hesitate. She slipped it onto her finger.

As soon as the ring touched her skin, she felt it—a sharp jolt, as if something had connected, something that had been missing for a long time. Her vision blurred for a moment, and she staggered back, feeling as though the ground beneath her feet had shifted. The room spun, and for a moment, she couldn't breathe. The air had grown thick, suffocating, pressing against her chest like a weight.

Lily gasped, her heart pounding violently as she fought for control. She yanked the ring from her finger and tossed it back into the box, but the sensation lingered. The weight in the air didn't lift, and the room remained suffocating, oppressive.

She looked down at her hand, trembling. There was a faint, dark mark where the ring had touched her skin, almost like a bruise. A deep, shadowy imprint, as though the ring had left something behind. Something she couldn't quite grasp.

The whisper came again, louder this time, a low murmur that

seemed to vibrate in her bones. She couldn't make out the words, but the tone was unmistakable—a warning. The feeling of being watched, of being hunted, returned with full force, and Lily's skin prickled with fear.

She slammed the lid shut on the box, her hands shaking violently. She stepped back, gasping for breath, but it was too late. The storm outside had found its way inside her house, and the shadows, the whispers—they were just beginning.

In the distance, she thought she heard the faintest sound—a footstep. Then another. The creaking of the floorboards.

And then, silence.

But it was the silence that terrified her most. Something was waiting in the shadows, just beyond her reach. And now, Lily knew, it was no longer a question of what was in the box.

It was what the box had brought with it.

16

The False Alarm

The rain had turned into a relentless downpour, thick sheets of water battering the windows, drumming a constant rhythm on the roof above. Lily stared at the phone in her hand, the screen glowing in the dim light of the living room. It had been just minutes since she received the message. The first one had come out of nowhere, and then a second, even more urgent one, followed quickly after.

There is no time. You must leave now.

It was a text, but there was something unsettling about it. No name. No number. Just a cryptic message. Lily's pulse quickened as she glanced around the room. The silence in the house felt suffocating, as though the walls themselves were holding their breath. Outside, the storm raged on, a thunderous roar that seemed to echo her rising sense of dread.

She had been sitting on the couch, trying to clear her head, trying to process the strange events of the past few days—the box, the ring, the feeling of something watching her, something sinister lurking just beyond the edge of her perception. But now, with the message flashing on her phone, that uneasy feeling had deepened into something darker, more pressing.

Lily ran her thumb over the screen, scanning the words again. Leave now. But leave where? The house was already dark, the power flickering as the storm continued its assault on the world outside. She swallowed hard, considering her options. She could call the police, but that would mean revealing just how much she had been keeping to herself, how many strange occurrences had been happening. She had no clear answers, only questions. And what if the message was nothing more than a cruel joke? What if there was nothing to fear?

But what if there was?

She stood abruptly, pacing the room as a feeling of vertigo crept over her. The walls seemed to close in, the shadows growing longer, as though the house itself were growing more oppressive by the second. The phone buzzed again, and Lily jumped, almost dropping it in surprise.

It's already too late. They're coming for you.

Her breath caught in her throat, a cold shiver creeping down her spine. The words echoed in her mind, reverberating like a warning bell. They're coming for you. Who? Who could possibly know she was here? And why now? She hadn't told anyone about the box, the ring, the unsettling events that had plagued her over the past few days. She hadn't even told her closest friend, Emma, about what was happening. She hadn't wanted to sound paranoid, to make anyone think she was losing her mind.

But now, the message felt like a confirmation of something much worse.

Lily quickly glanced around the room, her eyes falling on the front door. She thought she saw a shadow move outside the frosted window—just a brief flicker, as if someone had passed by, but when she strained her eyes to focus, there was nothing. The darkness beyond the glass remained undisturbed. But the sense of being watched had returned, creeping into her thoughts like an unwelcome intruder.

Her phone buzzed again, and this time, she didn't hesitate. She answered it, her hand shaking slightly as she held the device to her ear.

"Hello?" Her voice was strained, thin with tension, barely above a whisper.

There was silence on the other end for a long moment, just the soft static of a bad connection. Then, a voice—a low, rasping whisper—came through the line.

"Lily," the voice said, and her blood ran cold. It wasn't a voice she recognized, but it carried an unnerving familiarity, like a distant memory she couldn't quite place. "It's already begun. You have to leave now. They won't stop. They're already here."

Lily's heart raced, her breath catching in her throat. Her eyes darted to the windows, her pulse pounding in her ears. Something was wrong. This wasn't a joke. This wasn't a prank call. Whoever was on the other end knew her name—knew something about her. And now, they were warning her.

But warning her from what? Who were "they," and what was coming for her?

"What do you want from me?" Lily's voice broke, the question slipping from her lips before she could stop it. The words felt foolish, desperate, but they tumbled out all the same.

The voice on the other end let out a low, guttural laugh that sent a chill down her spine.

"There's no time for questions, Lily. You'll understand soon enough. But if you want to survive, you need to leave now. Go to the old church. The one at the edge of town. It's the only place you'll be safe. Do you understand?"

The voice faded with the words, and before Lily could respond, the call dropped. The line went dead, leaving her standing in the middle of the room, her breath coming in short, shallow gasps. She stared at the phone, her thoughts a whirlwind of confusion and fear. The old church. Why the church? What was it about the place that would keep her safe?

But then another thought struck her: What if this was a trap?

Lily's hand trembled as she set the phone down on the coffee table, her mind racing. If the voice was right, if something—or someone—was really coming for her, then she needed to act fast. She couldn't stay here, not with the house feeling as though it were closing in around her. But at the same time, the thought of walking into the storm, of heading to an unfamiliar place in the dead of night, made her stomach turn with dread.

The phone buzzed again.

It's not too late to run. But you have to move now. They're already watching you.

Lily jumped, her breath catching in her throat. Who was watching her? And how did they know where she was? Every instinct in her body screamed at her to stay put, to lock the doors, to protect herself. But the voice on the phone had been clear—they're already here. Whoever "they" were, they had found her. And they wouldn't stop until they had what they wanted.

She could hear her heart pounding in her chest as she crossed the room to the door. The house felt eerily quiet now, the ticking of the clock on the wall loud in the silence, as though time itself had slowed. She reached for the handle, her fingers cold against the metal. She hesitated for just a moment, her mind clouded with indecision, before she opened the door.

The wind hit her face like a slap, cold and biting, and the rain immediately soaked her through, but she didn't hesitate. She had no time to think. She had to go. Now.

Lily stepped outside, her feet sinking into the soft mud as she made her way down the porch steps. The path leading out of her yard was slick and treacherous, the shadows of the trees stretching unnaturally long in the light of the streetlamps. The air was thick with the scent of wet earth, but she couldn't shake the feeling that something was wrong—something was watching her.

Her breath came in shallow gasps as she hurried toward the edge of town, where the old church sat on a hill, its steeple looming against the night sky. Every step she took seemed to echo in the stillness, the sound magnified by the heavy rain. She glanced over her shoulder, certain she had seen a figure moving in the distance, but when she looked again, there was nothing. Just the endless stretch of empty road, the dark silhouette of the town behind her.

And yet, the feeling that she was being followed refused to leave.

The church loomed ahead, its silhouette growing larger with each step. But as she neared the gates, a new thought began to creep into her mind. What if this was a mistake? What if the voice had been leading her here for a reason other than safety?

And then, just as she reached the door, the air seemed to shift again. A strange chill crept over her, and she felt a sudden, overwhelming sense of dread. Something was wrong. She wasn't alone.

Lily pushed open the heavy wooden door and stepped inside, the smell of damp stone filling her nostrils. The door slammed shut behind her with a deafening bang, and the church went dark.

She was no longer sure if she was running toward safety—or walking right into the heart of her own nightmare.

17

The Waiting Room

The church had felt eerily quiet when Lily entered. It was a small, old building, its stone walls worn with age, the faint scent of mildew lingering in the air. The storm outside had drowned out any other sounds, leaving her alone with the beating of her own heart. The door slammed shut behind her, sending a jolt through her, and the darkness seemed to press in from every angle.

She hesitated by the door for a moment, the wetness of her clothes clinging uncomfortably to her skin, before pushing forward into the church's interior. The floor creaked under her feet as she walked cautiously into the nave, the faint flicker of candlelight illuminating the stone pews arranged in neat rows.

There was no one else here. The silence was overwhelming, more suffocating than comforting. She had expected the church to be empty, but something in her gut told her that there was more to it than that. It was as though the emptiness was intentional, a set-up designed to make her feel more alone than she had ever felt before.

Lily's breath was uneven, her pulse quickening with each step. The last message, the ominous warning, echoed in her mind: It's already too late. They're coming for you.

She pressed her hand against the back of a pew, the wood cold beneath her fingers, and looked up toward the altar. A single candle burned there, its flame flickering with a strange intensity, as though it were alive—alive with some purpose she couldn't understand. She felt drawn to it, as if it were a signal, a beacon of sorts, but there was a strange sense of reluctance that pulled her in the opposite direction.

It was then that she noticed the hallway leading off to the side of the altar, dimly lit by a single hanging light. There was something about the hallway, the shadows lurking just beyond the light, that made her pause. Was it always there? She had never noticed it before. Her instincts screamed at her to leave— to turn around and walk out of the church—but she knew that would be futile. She couldn't run forever. And something, something in the back of her mind, told her that whatever was waiting for her wasn't outside. It was in here.

With her heart hammering in her chest, Lily walked toward the hallway. The sound of her footsteps echoed far too loudly in the cavernous space, and the air around her seemed to grow heavier with each passing moment. She reached the hallway and hesitated at the threshold, her eyes scanning the narrow corridor. It was unsettlingly quiet, and the air felt stale and unused.

The hallway led to a single door at the end. It was an old wooden door, its paint peeling and chipped, as if it hadn't been opened in years. She had no idea why, but she was drawn to it. Something about that door promised answers, or at the very least, some kind of truth. She had to know what was behind it.

Her fingers brushed against the handle, cool and smooth to the touch. A jolt of electricity shot up her spine, and for a moment, she wanted to turn back, to run as fast as her legs would carry her. But then, the silence grew unbearable, the weight of the air suffocating her. She had no choice. She needed to open the door.

With a deep breath, Lily turned the handle and pushed the door open.

The room beyond was nothing like what she had imagined. It was a small, square room, completely bare except for a single chair in the center. The chair was old-fashioned, made of dark wood, and it looked out of place in the otherwise desolate space. The walls were bare, save for a single, large clock hanging on one wall, its hands frozen at precisely 12:00. The clock's ticking was absent, the time suspended in some strange, timeless state.

Lily stepped into the room, and as she did, the door behind her slammed shut, causing her to jump in shock. She turned quickly, but the door wouldn't budge. It was locked. Panic surged in her chest as she rattled the handle, but it was no use. She was trapped.

Her breath came in shallow gasps now, the oppressive silence almost too much to bear. She turned back to the room, to the chair in the center, and to the strange stillness that filled it. Something was wrong. It was as if the room itself had been waiting for her.

The chair was inviting in a way she couldn't explain. It beckoned her. Without fully understanding why, Lily walked toward it. Her feet moved on their own accord, as if something invisible was guiding her. When she reached the chair, she stopped for a moment, staring at it.

It looked comfortable. Too comfortable. The urge to sit in it was overwhelming, and she couldn't fight it. She sat down slowly, cautiously, as if she were testing the waters of some deep, uncharted ocean.

The moment her body made contact with the seat, a chill ran through her. It wasn't cold, exactly—it was more like a shift in the air, a movement of something unseen. The atmosphere around her seemed to change, thickening in a way she couldn't explain.

And then the clock began to tick.

It was faint at first, the sound so soft she wasn't sure if she had imagined it. But then it grew louder, faster, and more insistent. Tick. Tick. Tick. The sound echoed in the room, reverberating against the walls and bouncing around her mind.

What is this place? Lily thought frantically, her heart racing. The room felt colder now, though the temperature hadn't changed. It was as if the air itself were closing in on her, pushing her into the chair, forcing her to remain there.

Her gaze moved to the walls again, but she couldn't see anything new. The clock ticked on, louder and louder, each second dragging on with unbearable weight. And then, without warning, the door behind her opened.

Lily whipped around in shock, her breath catching in her throat. Standing in the doorway was a figure. At first, it was too dark to make out any details, but as the figure stepped into the room, the light from the hallway illuminated them. It was a man, dressed in a black suit, his face obscured by a shadowed hood. He didn't speak, but his presence was suffocating, as though his very being filled the room, crushing her under the weight of its intensity.

Lily's mouth went dry. She opened her mouth to speak, to demand answers, but no words came. The figure didn't move, only stood there, watching her with eyes she couldn't see.

The clock ticked louder now, as if counting down. The silence between them stretched on, suffocating, the seconds dragging like hours.

And then, the man's voice came. Low. Soft. But carrying a weight of finality.

"You're in the waiting room, Lily."

Her pulse quickened at the sound of her name, and her stomach turned. She was paralyzed in the chair, unable to speak, unable to move. The air grew heavier, and her mind reeled, trying to make sense of what was happening.

"Waiting for what?" she finally managed to ask, her voice trembling with fear.

The man stepped closer, and for the first time, Lily could see his face—a face she didn't recognize, yet somehow felt familiar, like a shadow from a dream. He tilted his head slightly, as if considering her question.

"You're waiting for the truth," he said, his voice so calm it sent shivers down her spine.

Lily's mind raced, her body still frozen in place. She had no idea what this man meant, but she understood one thing—whatever was happening here, whatever this room was, it wasn't going to let her leave until she had faced it.

18

The Unsolved Puzzle

The sound of rain pounding against the windows was the first thing Lily noticed as she regained consciousness. It wasn't a gentle rain. It was a relentless, drumming assault of water. She opened her eyes slowly, the world coming into focus in fragments, like an old photograph being pieced together. The room was dim, but there was a soft light in the corner, where a solitary lamp cast long shadows against the walls.

She sat up with a gasp, her hands pressing into the cold wooden floor. She didn't know where she was. Her body felt heavy, as if weighted by something unseen, and her mind was clouded with a fog of confusion. The last thing she remembered was the strange man in the church hallway—the one who had spoken of truth, of waiting—and then the world had gone black.

The room around her was unlike anything she'd ever seen. It was a small, sparse space, the walls lined with bookshelves filled with old, dusty volumes. At the center of the room was a large wooden table, its surface cluttered with papers, odd tools, and strange objects that Lily couldn't identify. A puzzle, its pieces scattered across the table, caught her eye. A puzzle, she thought, but it wasn't just any puzzle. This one felt... different.

Her pulse quickened as she stood shakily, her legs unsteady beneath her. She stumbled toward the table, her hand brushing against the pieces of the puzzle. They were scattered haphazardly, as though someone had been in the middle of putting it together and then abandoned it. She leaned over the table, her fingers moving over the pieces, instinctively trying to fit them together. But something was wrong. The pieces didn't fit. No matter how hard she tried, they wouldn't come together.

And then she noticed something else—something that made her breath catch in her throat.

The pieces weren't just shaped to fit together. They were... different. Some of them felt cold to the touch, others warm, as if they were alive. The colors on them shifted and swirled in a way that shouldn't have been possible. And the patterns—they didn't make sense. It was as though the puzzle was constantly changing, shifting in ways that defied logic.

Lily stepped back, her heart pounding. There was a deeper meaning to this puzzle, one she wasn't yet able to understand, but she knew it was somehow connected to everything that had been happening to her. The strange events, the cryptic messages, the man in the church—all of it led here, to this room, to this table, to this puzzle.

She glanced around the room again, her eyes searching for any hint of what was going on. But the walls remained silent, the shelves offering no answers. The air in the room felt thick, oppressive, as if the very atmosphere were waiting for her to make the next move.

A sudden noise broke the silence—soft at first, like a whisper. Lily froze, her heart in her throat. She strained to listen, but the noise was gone. She shook her head, trying to dismiss the thought that had crossed her mind. It was just the house settling. She was imagining things.

But then the noise came again. This time, it was louder, unmistakable. A tapping sound. It was coming from the window.

Lily turned, her eyes searching the darkness beyond the rain-soaked glass. There was nothing there. Nothing but the swirling night and the rain pelting the window in violent streaks. She took a cautious step toward the window, her breath catching in her chest. What could it be?

Her hand reached for the curtain, and she yanked it open, the fabric rustling in the quiet room. She peered out into the night, her gaze scanning the empty street below. The tapping stopped the moment she looked outside.

Her pulse thudded in her ears. No one was there. The street was empty, dark and silent, save for the rain. But she couldn't shake the feeling that something was watching her, something out there, just beyond the edge of her sight.

Turning away from the window, she moved back toward the table. Her mind was spinning with questions, none of which she could answer. The puzzle seemed to mock her, the pieces refusing to fit together, the images on them elusive, constantly shifting.

She took a deep breath, trying to steady herself. This puzzle was a key. She could feel it in her bones. But what did it unlock?

Without thinking, she reached out and grabbed one of the pieces, holding it up to the light. The patterns on it were even more intricate than before, the colors shifting in strange, fluid motions. There was something haunting about the piece—a sense of familiarity, as though she had seen it before, or perhaps had always known it.

And then, without warning, the piece began to burn.

She gasped, pulling her hand back in shock. The piece was hot to the touch, radiating an intense warmth. She dropped it onto the table, watching as it sizzled, the colors on it swirling violently before it vanished into thin air.

Her heart raced, panic flooding her chest. What had just happened? What was that thing?

The room felt colder now, as though the temperature had dropped several degrees in an instant. She wrapped her arms around herself, trying to calm the tremors in her hands. But the unease was growing stronger, creeping into her bones. She wasn't alone in this room. Something else was here, something watching her every move.

Lily stumbled backward, her eyes scanning the room once again. The puzzle pieces had vanished. The table was now empty, the once-cluttered surface clean and bare. She blinked, her breath coming in short, sharp gasps. What was going on? Had she imagined the puzzle? Was it all in her mind?

No. She couldn't be imagining it. It had been real. The pieces, the shifting patterns, the burning—everything. It had been real.

Suddenly, the room grew darker, the light from the lamp flickering as if struggling to stay on. The shadows in the corners deepened, stretching like dark fingers, reaching toward her. A low hum filled the air, vibrating through her chest, making her heart race even faster.

The door to the room slammed shut, and the lights flickered one last time before going out completely, plunging her into darkness.

Lily's breath hitched, and for a moment, all she could hear was the pounding of her heart. She strained her ears, listening for any sound in the silence, but it was too quiet. It was as if the world had fallen into a deep, oppressive hush.

Then, from somewhere in the darkness, a voice spoke.

"Do you want to know the truth?"

Lily's body went rigid. The voice was soft, distant, but it was unmistakable. She could hear it in her bones, in her blood. It was the same voice from the church. The same man who had spoken to her in the hallway.

She turned, desperately searching for the source of the voice, but saw nothing. The shadows seemed to pulse with each word, stretching further into the room.

"The puzzle is a key," the voice continued, growing louder, closer. "But it is not just a puzzle of pieces. It is a puzzle of your mind. Of your past. You must solve it if you want to escape."

Lily's breath caught in her throat. She could feel the weight of the words sinking into her soul, heavy and unrelenting. What did it mean? What was she supposed to do?

A sudden flash of light illuminated the room. It was brief, like the flash of a camera, but in that instant, Lily saw it.

The puzzle. It was back on the table.

But now, the pieces had changed. They were no longer just strange, shifting shapes. They were faces—faces she recognized. Faces from her past. Faces of people she had known, people she had lost.

And in the center of the puzzle, there was one face that wasn't hers but was familiar in a way that made her stomach churn.

It was the man from the church.

19

The Unseen Killer

The night air was thick with tension, a suffocating stillness that pressed down on Lily's chest. She had barely slept, her mind swirling with the haunting images from the room—the puzzle, the faces, the man who had whispered to her from the shadows. But it was the feeling of being watched that kept her awake, the sensation that something—someone—was lurking just beyond her reach.

The house was quiet now, the only sound the occasional creak of the floorboards underfoot or the distant rustle of wind against the windows. But it wasn't a comforting silence. It was an unsettling quiet, as though the house itself was holding its breath, waiting for something to happen.

Lily stepped out of her bedroom, her bare feet cold against the hardwood floor. She moved down the narrow hallway, her senses on high alert. Every door, every corner felt like it was hiding something from her, something she couldn't see, couldn't understand. Her pulse quickened as she passed the bathroom, the kitchen, and the stairwell that led to the basement.

She stopped in front of the door to the living room. The dim light of the streetlamp outside barely filtered through the curtains, casting long shadows across the floor. Her hand hovered over the doorknob, and for a brief moment, she hesitated. The air in the house felt wrong, thick with something she couldn't explain. It was as though the walls were closing in on her, suffocating her from all sides.

But she couldn't ignore it any longer. She had to know.

With a deep breath, she turned the knob and stepped into the room.

The living room was empty, just as it had been when she left it hours ago. The old armchair in the corner, the dusty bookshelves, the fireplace—nothing had changed. But something was different. The room felt... off. There was an oppressive weight to the air, a heaviness that seemed to press against her chest.

She took a tentative step forward, her eyes scanning the space. Nothing moved. Nothing stirred.

But then, just as she was about to turn toward the door, something caught her eye—a glimmer of movement in the corner of the room, near the window. Her heart skipped a beat as she turned her head, her breath catching in her throat.

It was quick, too quick for her to fully process, but it was there. A shadow. A figure, barely visible, crouching low against the wall.

Her blood ran cold.

She didn't move. Didn't even breathe, afraid that any noise would alert the figure to her presence. The shadow didn't move either, but it was there—waiting, watching.

Lily's hand clenched into a fist, her nails digging into the skin of her palm. She forced herself to remain calm, to think. There had to be a logical explanation. It could have been a trick of the light. It could have been a shadow cast by the wind or something outside.

But the fear gnawing at her gut told her otherwise. The feeling in her chest told her this wasn't just a trick. Someone—or something—was in the room with her.

She took a slow step backward, her eyes never leaving the shadow. She had to get out of the room, had to get to the phone, had to call for help. But the more she moved, the more she felt the presence closing in, as if it were drawn to her every movement.

Her foot hit the edge of a table with a soft thud. She froze.

The shadow shifted.

Lily's breath caught in her throat, and a cold sweat broke out across her skin. The figure in the corner moved again, slower this time, deliberate. It was getting closer.

Without thinking, she turned and bolted for the door.

She was almost there—just a few more feet, just a few more steps—but then, out of the corner of her eye, she saw it. A flash of movement, a blur in the dark, and before she could react, something heavy slammed into her from behind.

She was thrown forward, her hands reaching out instinctively to break her fall, but the impact knocked the breath from her lungs. She hit the floor hard, pain shooting up her arms and into her chest.

Before she could gather her bearings, a cold hand gripped her wrist, pulling her back into the darkness. A voice, low and menacing, whispered in her ear.

"Don't scream."

The words sent a shock of terror through her, but she bit her lip to stifle the instinct to scream, to run. She couldn't let this person know how terrified she was. Not yet.

The hand on her wrist tightened, pulling her toward the center of the room. She could feel the heat of the stranger's body close to hers, could smell the faint scent of cologne mixed with sweat. It was a smell she didn't recognize, and yet, somehow, it felt familiar. Uncomfortably so.

Lily's mind raced, trying to come up with a plan, a way to escape. She had to think, had to act fast. She tried to twist her wrist free from the grip, but the hand was like a vice, unrelenting.

"Who are you?" she gasped, her voice trembling despite her best efforts to remain calm.

There was no answer at first. The figure didn't speak, didn't even acknowledge her question. Instead, they just pulled her further into the room, their grip never loosening.

Lily's heart was pounding in her chest. She had to get away. She had to do something.

She glanced around the room frantically, her eyes darting from one corner to another. And then, she saw it. A small, jagged object on the floor—a shard of broken glass from the vase she had knocked over earlier. It was just within her reach.

With every ounce of strength, Lily lunged for the shard, grabbing it with her free hand. She held it tight, the cold glass digging into her skin, as she twisted her body to face her attacker.

In one swift motion, she thrust the shard toward the figure, aiming for the hand that held her. The blade cut through the air, but the figure reacted just in time, jerking their hand back. The glass missed its mark, but it was enough to make them hesitate, enough to make them loosen their grip, just for a moment.

That was all Lily needed.

She yanked her wrist free and scrambled to her feet, her breath coming in ragged gasps. She turned to run, but before she could take more than a few steps, the figure was on her again, this time grabbing her by the hair and yanking her back with terrifying strength.

"Not so fast," the voice growled.

Lily's head spun as she struggled to break free. She could feel the panic rising in her throat, threatening to choke her. She had to escape. She couldn't let them catch her.

In the midst of the chaos, something flashed in her mind— the puzzle. The strange images, the shifting pieces, the faces. There had to be a connection. This man, this person, he was part of it. They were all part of it.

Her body was moving on autopilot now, fueled by sheer desperation. She twisted, kicked, and finally managed to break free from the stranger's grip. She staggered backward, trying to catch her breath, her heart hammering in her chest.

But the figure wasn't done. They lunged at her again, but this time, Lily was ready. She grabbed the first object she could find, a heavy brass lamp sitting on a nearby table, and swung it with all her strength.

The lamp connected with the figure's head with a sickening thud, and they collapsed to the floor, stunned.

For a moment, everything was still.

Lily's chest rose and fell with each labored breath as she stood over the motionless figure. She had done it. She had fought back. But the relief was fleeting, replaced quickly by a sense of dread.

She wasn't safe yet. She knew that now. Something far darker was at play here, and this—this man—was just a small part of it.

Lily's eyes flicked to the door, and without another moment's hesitation, she turned and ran, leaving the stranger behind, knowing that whatever was hunting her, it was far from finished.

20

The Box

Lily stood frozen in the dim light of the hallway, her pulse still racing from the events of the last few hours. Her hands were trembling, her mind in a whirlwind. What had just happened? Who was the stranger? And why did it feel like they weren't the only one hunting her?

She couldn't stay in the house any longer. She needed to get out, to find answers, to escape the suffocating grip of the shadows that seemed to follow her at every turn. But as she moved toward the door, something caught her eye.

The box.

It sat on the small wooden table near the entrance, waiting. Lily's throat went dry. She had seen it earlier, sitting innocuously on the table, tucked into the corner of the room. But she hadn't thought much of it at the time. It wasn't until now, in the aftermath of everything, that it seemed to take on a new, ominous meaning.

The box was old, the edges worn with age, its surface cracked and faded. There was no return address, no markings, nothing to indicate where it had come from or why it was here. Just a plain, unassuming box, no bigger than a shoebox, but to Lily, it felt like the center of everything.

She could feel its presence, the weight of it pressing against her chest as if it were somehow connected to all the things that had been happening. The strange figure in the house, the shadows in the corner of her vision, the inexplicable sense that something was terribly wrong. Everything had built up to this moment, to the unopened box.

Lily took a cautious step toward it, her feet heavy as if they were trying to resist the pull. The floor creaked beneath her, a sound that seemed far too loud in the stillness of the house. The box sat there, taunting her, daring her to open it.

She swallowed hard. Should she open it? Should she leave it alone? Everything inside her screamed to walk away, to ignore it, to not take one more step toward the nightmare that seemed to be unfolding around her. But at the same time, something inside her burned with curiosity, with the desperate need to know what was inside. Was it a clue? A warning? Or was it something far more dangerous?

The light from the hallway flickered, and for a brief moment, the shadows seemed to stretch unnaturally long, curling like tendrils of darkness. Lily's hand trembled as she reached out, her fingers brushing the cold, rough surface of the box.

It felt... strange. Almost alive, as if it were pulsing with some unseen force. Her breath caught in her throat, and she hesitated for a moment. But the urge to find out what was inside overtook her. She had to know.

With a sharp exhale, she lifted the lid.

At first, she saw nothing but darkness. The box was empty. But then, her eyes adjusted, and she saw it. A small, crumpled piece of paper, buried beneath the fabric that lined the inside of the box.

Lily's heart raced as she reached in, her fingers trembling as she pulled the paper free. It was old, yellowed with age, and the edges were frayed as if it had been handled countless times. She unfolded it carefully, her eyes scanning the words that were written in a hurried, jagged scrawl.

"They're watching. They know you're close."

The words sent a shiver down her spine, and she felt a cold sweat break out on her forehead. The message was cryptic, but the implications were terrifying. Who was watching? What did they know? And how close was she to whatever this... this thing was that had been following her?

Her thoughts swirled as she tried to make sense of the note, but the more she thought about it, the more her mind refused to connect the dots. She had to get out of the house, but something told her that wasn't enough. She needed answers. She needed to understand what was happening to her, why she was being targeted.

And then, as if on cue, she heard it.

A sound, faint at first, but unmistakable. A tap. A soft tap on the door, like the lightest knock, barely audible. It was followed by another, then another, until it became a rhythmic tapping, a steady, persistent beat.

Lily froze. The hairs on the back of her neck stood on end as she listened intently. The knocking came from behind the door, coming from the other side of the room, the place where she had just been standing moments ago.

Her breath hitched, and her grip on the box tightened. Who could be knocking at this hour? No one knew she was here. No one except the stranger. And if they were here...

No. She couldn't think like that. It was just her mind playing tricks on her. She had to stay calm.

But the knocking didn't stop. It was growing louder, more insistent, and Lily's heart began to pound in her chest, each beat growing faster and harder. Her instincts screamed at her to run, but her feet refused to move. Her eyes were fixed on the door, her breath shallow as she waited for whatever was on the other side to make itself known.

And then, in an instant, the door rattled.

The knob turned, a soft, almost imperceptible click sounding in the stillness of the room. Lily's blood ran cold. The door wasn't locked. She hadn't locked it.

The tapping stopped.

For a moment, there was nothing. Just the empty, oppressive silence that seemed to swallow the room whole. Lily's mind raced, each thought coming faster than the last. Should she hide? Should she run? Should she open the door and face whatever waited on the other side?

Before she could make a decision, the door creaked open by itself, just a crack, enough to see the shadow on the other side, but not enough to reveal who—or what—was there.

Her stomach twisted in knots as she tried to make sense of what she was seeing. The shadow was tall, too tall, and it moved unnaturally, like a figure that wasn't quite solid, shifting in ways that defied reason.

And then, the voice. A low, raspy whisper that slithered through the crack in the door, sending a cold shiver through her spine.

"You opened the box."

Lily's heart skipped a beat, her mind going blank with terror. She didn't answer. She couldn't answer.

The door creaked again, louder this time, and Lily backed away slowly, her eyes fixed on the shadow. The figure didn't move, didn't speak again, but she could feel its presence, its cold, oppressive weight bearing down on her.

She needed to leave. Now.

Without a second thought, Lily turned and ran, her footsteps echoing loudly in the house as she sprinted down the hallway. But as she reached the front door, she froze.

It was locked.

The deadbolt, the knob—everything was locked tight, as though someone had sealed her inside.

The knocking started again, louder this time, pounding against the door like an unstoppable force. The walls seemed to close in around her, the darkness pressing against her chest.

Lily's pulse raced as she scrambled to find something— anything—that could break the hold of the locked door. Her hands trembled as she pulled at the handle, but the door wouldn't budge.

The shadows were closing in.

Then, as if the house itself had decided to join in the horror, the lights flickered.

And then, everything went black.

21

The Vanish

Lily jolted awake, her eyes snapping open to the unfamiliar surroundings. She had been running, hadn't she? The locked door, the knocking, the shadows closing in around her—it had all been so real. But now, as she sat up, she found herself in a small, dimly lit room. Her surroundings were minimal: a single wooden chair in the corner, a small table with a lamp that flickered as though it were struggling to stay on, and the faint scent of old paper and dust in the air. The walls were bare, the floor wooden and creaky beneath her.

Her heart raced in her chest as she tried to make sense of what had happened. The last thing she remembered was the lights going out, the feeling of the house closing in on her, and the door that wouldn't open. How had she ended up here? Was this real? Or was it another trap? Another layer to the nightmare she'd been trapped in for what felt like forever?

She stood up slowly, the room tilting slightly around her as she regained her balance. Her head throbbed with a dull ache, and her hands still trembled from the shock of whatever had happened. Her fingers brushed against the back of her neck, her skin sticky with sweat. She glanced down and realized she was still wearing the same clothes—mud-streaked jeans and a t-shirt, her shoes scuffed and worn.

She took a step toward the door, her breath hitching as she noticed a thin, almost imperceptible crack in the wood. It was a small thing, but it was enough to send a chill through her. Someone had been here. Someone was watching.

Lily hesitated, her hand hovering over the doorknob. She was already halfway to the door when the thought hit her—why hadn't anyone come to check on her? She had no idea how long she had been in this room, or if she was even alone. There had to be someone nearby, someone who had brought her here, someone who had answers.

But as she slowly twisted the doorknob, a sound outside stopped her cold. A faint, almost inaudible voice, barely a whisper, but unmistakably clear.

"It's not too late."

Lily froze, her breath caught in her throat. The voice had been close—so close that it could have come from the other side of the door. She pressed her ear against the wood, straining to hear more, but the whisper had faded, leaving nothing but silence. Her mind raced. Who had said that? And what did it mean?

She turned the knob slowly, cautiously, and pushed the door open just enough to slip through. The hallway outside was dim, lit only by the soft glow of a single bulb hanging from the ceiling. It was eerily quiet, the kind of silence that felt like it was pressing in on her from all sides.

The walls here, like the room she had just left, were bare, almost clinical in their emptiness. No windows, no decorations—just the sterile hum of the light and the faint scent of mildew in the air. There was nothing to indicate where she was, how she had gotten there, or what the purpose of this place was.

Lily's gaze flicked to the end of the hallway. There was a door, a metal one, standing ajar, a sliver of light spilling out from inside. Something about it pulled her, like a magnet drawing her in, but also warning her to stay away. Her instincts screamed at her to turn back, to go the other way, but the whispering voice echoed in her mind.

It's not too late.

She had to know what it meant. She had to find out who was behind this—who was playing these games with her.

Her footsteps were nearly silent as she approached the door, her body tense and ready to spring into action if she needed to. The closer she got, the more the air seemed to grow thick with anticipation. She could feel the hairs on the back of her neck rise, the prickling sensation of being watched, of being drawn into something she couldn't yet comprehend.

When she reached the door, she hesitated for only a moment before pushing it open.

Inside was a small office, stark and sterile, much like the hallway outside. A single desk sat in the center of the room, papers stacked haphazardly on top. A filing cabinet stood against the far wall, and a lone chair sat in front of the desk, as if waiting for someone to take a seat. But it was the man standing at the far side of the room that caught Lily's attention.

He was tall, his features sharp and angular, with a coldness in his eyes that made her blood run cold. His suit was immaculate, black with a subtle sheen, and his tie was perfectly knotted. His face was unreadable, as though he had been practicing the art of indifference for years. But it wasn't his appearance that made her stomach twist with dread. It was the way he looked at her—like he knew everything about her, like he was expecting her.

"You've been running for a long time, Lily," he said, his voice calm, almost too calm. It sent a ripple of unease down her spine. "But running won't help you now."

Lily took a step back, her eyes scanning the room, searching for an escape route. There was nowhere to go, no windows to jump through, no back door to slip through unnoticed. The man's gaze never wavered, his eyes tracking her every move.

"Who are you?" Lily demanded, her voice shaking despite her best efforts to keep it steady. "What do you want from me?"

The man smiled faintly, the expression cold and calculating. "What I want from you? Nothing. You see, you're the one who's been asking all the questions, Lily. You're the one who's been trying to uncover the truth."

Lily's pulse quickened. "I'm not the one who's been hiding things. I'm not the one who—"

He cut her off with a sharp motion of his hand. "No, you're not. But you're the one who's gotten too close. Too close to the truth. And now, there are consequences."

She swallowed hard, trying to keep her composure. She was out of her depth, and she knew it. There was something far darker at play here than she could have imagined.

"I don't know what you're talking about," she said, her voice strained. "I'm just trying to understand why all of this is happening."

The man's smile faded. "You don't need to understand, Lily. You just need to accept it. Because the truth is something you can't unlearn. And once you've seen it, once you know... you become a witness. But what happens to witnesses in this game, Lily? They vanish."

Lily's heart skipped a beat. "What do you mean? What are you going to do to me?"

The man stepped forward, his movements fluid and controlled. "Oh, nothing that hasn't been done before. You see, you've become a part of something much bigger than yourself. And you're not the first to try to escape it. Many have tried. But they all disappear in the end."

A wave of dread washed over Lily, and for the first time, she felt the true weight of the situation. She wasn't just a victim. She was a part of something. She didn't know what it was yet, but she was right in the middle of it, and it was closing in around her.

Before she could respond, the man's eyes flicked to the door behind her. Lily turned just in time to see the shadow of someone else slip into the room. She didn't have time to react before the second figure lunged forward, grabbing her by the arm.

The last thing she saw was the man's cold smile as everything went black.

22

The Vanishing Witness

Lily's body jerked as she was yanked from the darkness, her senses snapping back with brutal clarity. The air was thick, humid, and smelled of stale dust and old wood, but it wasn't the scent that had her attention. No, it was the sharp pain in her wrist where someone's hand gripped her, and the cold that crawled up her spine.

She opened her eyes, but the room around her spun in a disorienting blur. Her head throbbed, her vision swam, but she managed to blink through the haze, trying to piece together her surroundings. She was no longer in the sterile office. Instead, she found herself in a cramped, dimly lit room, the kind of place that looked as though it hadn't been touched in years.

The walls were peeling, the floor covered in layers of dust, and the only furniture was an old chair in front of a small, wooden table. Her breath caught in her throat when she realized what was in front of her—a man's face. Not the cold man from the office, but someone else. Someone familiar. Her chest tightened.

The man's face was ghostly pale, his eyes sunken into dark, hollow sockets. He looked like someone who hadn't seen daylight in months. His hair was unkempt, his clothes tattered and faded. He stared at her with an expression that she couldn't quite place—intensity, fear, perhaps something worse. His lips parted, but before he could say anything, the door creaked behind her.

Lily's heart skipped. She recognized the sound. The click of a door opening slowly, the heavy, deliberate pace of footsteps that followed.

"Leave her be," a voice ordered from the doorway. Lily's breath caught as she recognized the voice—smooth, too calm, the same voice that had spoken to her in the sterile office. The man who had taken control. The one who knew too much.

The man standing over her straightened, but he didn't turn around. He stood frozen, his hand gripping the arm of the chair like it was a lifeline, as though unsure whether he should obey the command.

"No," the man said, his voice low and strained. "I'm not letting her go. Not yet."

Lily's mind raced, trying to piece together what was happening, what she was doing in this forgotten room, and why the man was holding her here. But there was no time for her to think. The door clicked closed with a finality that made her pulse quicken.

"Get up," the voice behind her said, sharper now. The command wasn't a question, and Lily knew she had no choice but to obey.

With a swift pull, the man grabbed her wrist, dragging her to her feet. The world around her spun again, but she fought to stay grounded, her eyes darting around for any way out. The door. The window, which was barely more than a cracked opening high in the wall. But there was no easy way out. No visible escape.

Her captor guided her forward, pushing her through the narrow hallway that led to another room, this one slightly larger, though still suffocating. She could hear the faint sound of breathing behind her, and she turned her head, briefly meeting the eyes of the man who had tried to hold her.

"Do you know who I am?" the man rasped. His voice was barely audible, but there was an edge to it that sent chills running up Lily's spine.

She tried to focus, but the adrenaline and fear blurred her thoughts. "Who are you?" she whispered, still too weak to put up a fight.

The man's lips quivered slightly. "I—I don't know how much time we have." He looked toward the door. "He's going to— he's going to do something. Something that... I don't know if you'll survive."

Her mind reeled at his words, a cold, terrible truth beginning to sink in. She wasn't alone in this. The other man, the one who had been watching her, had plans for them both. And whatever those plans were, she wasn't sure she would make it out alive.

Before Lily could process it further, the door to the larger room creaked open, and the man behind her urged her inside.

The room was dim, lit only by the faint glow of a flickering light bulb. The air felt even thicker here, as though it had been sealed off from the outside world. The walls were lined with papers—notes, photographs, and maps covered every inch, each pinned up with pins and strings, creating a tangled web of information. It looked like a detective's wall, only there were no names, no clear connections. Just chaos.

And then, at the center of the chaos, was the man who had been pulling the strings all along. The one who controlled this place, who spoke with authority, who had ordered the others around.

He stood at the far side of the room, his back to her, staring out of the grimy window. He hadn't moved when she entered, but she felt the weight of his gaze, even though he wasn't looking at her.

Lily's heart pounded in her chest. She wanted to run, to escape, but she knew she couldn't. She was trapped.

The man in front of her, the one who had been holding her captive, spoke again, his voice barely above a whisper. "You've been asking too many questions. Too many things you shouldn't have known. You shouldn't have gone this far."

Lily swallowed hard, trying to steady herself. "Who are you? What do you want from me?"

The man paused for a long moment before answering, his voice low and grim. "You don't understand. You never did. This isn't about you, Lily. It never was. It's about what you saw. What you know."

Lily's mind reeled. She was starting to feel the weight of the truth bearing down on her. Something had been hidden, something buried so deep that even she couldn't comprehend it. But whatever it was, it was dangerous. Too dangerous for her to uncover.

The man finally turned to face her. His eyes were cold, unfeeling. "You saw too much. Now, you'll have to disappear."

Lily's blood ran cold. The words echoed in her mind, reverberating like the hum of electricity. "Disappear?"

The man nodded, stepping forward with an air of finality. "You can't unsee what you saw. So, you have to go. Leave. Leave now, and never come back."

Lily's heart raced. She could hear the urgency in his voice, feel the threat that hung in the air. And suddenly, it all clicked. She had seen something, heard something that she wasn't meant to. Something that was too dangerous for anyone to know.

But there was something else. The room, the walls, the chaos—it was all wrong. She wasn't meant to be here. This wasn't where she was supposed to be. Something had changed.

The man stepped closer, his hand reaching out as though to grab her. But before he could, the door behind her swung open with a force that sent it crashing against the wall.

"Lily," a voice called, a voice she recognized—shaky, desperate.

It was him. The man who had been trying to save her. The one who had warned her.

"You have to go. Now!"

Lily didn't think. She just ran.

Her feet pounded against the floor, the world blurring as she tore through the hall, the sound of footsteps chasing her from behind. She reached the door, yanked it open, and slammed it behind her. For a moment, she just stood there, breathless, her heart hammering against her chest.

But then, the silence fell. The room, the man, the chaos—it was all behind her. She had run. She had escaped.

For now.

But something was wrong.

Something still wasn't right.

And as Lily fled into the unknown, the feeling in her gut told her that this was far from over.

23

The Unopened Box

The heavy rain lashed against the windows as the storm raged outside. A cold draft seeped through the cracks in the walls, but Lily barely noticed. She was too focused on the box sitting in the middle of her living room. It was small—no larger than a shoebox—and wrapped in brown paper with no markings, no name, no return address. Just a simple, plain box that had appeared on her doorstep earlier that morning. She hadn't heard anyone approach, hadn't seen any sign of who had left it. It was as though it had simply materialized out of thin air.

Her heart pounded in her chest as she stood frozen in front of it. It had been hours since she found it, and in all that time, she had not once dared to touch it. She couldn't. Something about it felt wrong—unnatural. The weight of it was odd, too heavy for its size. And yet, no matter how much she tried to ignore it, it was there, in the center of her world, demanding her attention. Its presence was like a silent scream in the back of her mind, a nagging sensation that wouldn't go away.

She couldn't remember the last time she'd felt so utterly helpless.

Lily glanced over her shoulder toward the closed door of her apartment, half-expecting someone to burst through at any moment. The last few days had been a blur of confusion, fear, and unanswered questions. She had no idea what she had seen, what she had been part of, or who was trying to silence her. But every instinct told her that whoever was behind all of this had left the box for a reason. She just didn't know what that reason was—or how much danger it posed.

Her mind wandered back to the night she'd escaped the strange, locked room. The man who had tried to warn her, the one who had been there with her, he was gone now. Had he survived? Was he even real? It seemed impossible to know what to believe anymore, and she hadn't spoken to anyone about the events she'd witnessed. The things she'd seen, heard, felt—they all felt like a dream, like fragments of a nightmare that refused to let go.

But the box... the box was real.

She took a step forward, her breath shallow, her hand trembling as she reached for it. The storm outside seemed to intensify as she moved, the howling wind rattling the windows and the occasional flash of lightning illuminating the room in stark, jagged streaks. It was as if the storm itself was trying to warn her, to make her stop. But she couldn't.

Her fingers brushed the edge of the box, and she jumped back, a shock of panic surging through her. The box didn't move. It didn't shift. It didn't even make a sound, but somehow, it felt... alive. She shook her head, trying to dispel the irrational thought. It was just a box. It was just a damn box.

But still, she couldn't shake the feeling that it had been waiting for her.

Lily stepped back again, wiping her damp palms against her jeans. She felt like she was losing her grip on reality. Maybe she was just paranoid. Maybe this was all in her head, the product of too much fear, too much uncertainty. But there was something about the way the box sat there—its stillness, its calm—that made her believe it was anything but ordinary.

Taking a deep breath, Lily crouched down and picked up the box. Her fingers curled around it, and for a brief moment, she thought she heard a faint thrum, like the beating of a heart. But when she glanced down, the box was still, silent, almost... serene. Her heart skipped a beat. Was it her imagination? Or was there something more to it?

She set the box carefully on the table in front of her and ran her hands over the paper. The texture was rough, almost like burlap, but not quite. The edges were frayed, and the paper itself seemed to have an odd sheen, almost as if it had been coated with something.

Lily took a deep breath, fighting the instinct to put it down and run. She had to know what was inside. Whatever this was, it had to be uncovered.

With trembling hands, she unwrapped the paper, the sound of it tearing loudly in the silence of the room. As the last of the paper fell away, her stomach twisted into a tight knot.

Inside the box, nestled in layers of crinkled tissue paper, was a small object. It was a book. A leather-bound book, its cover dark and aged, its edges worn, as if it had been handled countless times before. The leather had the distinct look of something ancient, something from another era. Its surface was almost unnaturally smooth, but there were no markings, no title, no sign of where it had come from or who had created it. It was completely unremarkable in every way, save for its presence.

Lily felt a chill crawl up her spine as she picked it up, her fingers brushing over the cover. The weight of it felt... wrong. Not physically heavy, but emotionally heavy, as though it carried the weight of untold stories, of secrets too dark to be spoken aloud.

What was this?

She flipped the book open, her hands trembling as she scanned the first page.

There were no words.

Just empty space. The page was blank. But as she turned to the next, the same thing. Nothing. It was a book filled with blank pages. Her breath quickened. She flipped through every single page, her heart racing, but each page was just as empty as the one before. It was the same on every single page, as though the book had been written with invisible ink. There was no trace of what it had been meant to contain.

But then, when she reached the very last page, something shifted.

A faint scribble appeared at the bottom corner of the page. It was small, almost too small to read, but it was there—just barely visible—as if the words had only just started to appear. Her hands shook as she leaned closer, straining to make out the writing.

And then, the words became clear.

"They are watching. They always have been. You will know who they are when the time comes."

Lily froze, her pulse quickening as the room seemed to close in around her. The words seemed to burn into her mind, leaving a dark imprint that wouldn't go away.

She slammed the book shut, the sound echoing through the apartment. Her breath came in ragged gasps, the air thick with fear.

The storm outside raged louder now, the wind howling, the rain hammering against the windows as though trying to get in. Lily felt a sudden urge to leave, to run, but she couldn't. She felt like she was trapped, as though the very walls of her apartment had closed in around her.

The words from the book repeated in her mind, over and over again. They are watching.

She could almost hear them—whispers from the corners of the room, from the shadows in the hallway. Something was here. Something was waiting. She couldn't stay in the apartment any longer.

With trembling hands, she stuffed the book back into the box, re-wrapped it hastily, and stumbled to the door. She didn't know where she was going. She didn't know who she could trust. But she had to leave.

She had to get out.

And yet, as she stepped into the hallway and turned the key in the lock, she felt it. The presence. The eyes on her.

The watchers. They were here. They had always been here. And now, they knew she had the book.

But it was too late to stop now.

Lily ran.

24

The Alarm

The city was eerily quiet as Lily stepped into the street, her breath coming out in short, frantic bursts. The rain had tapered off to a light drizzle, but the air still felt thick, suffocating. It pressed down on her chest, making it harder to breathe. She had no destination in mind, only the desperate need to get away, to put as much distance between herself and the box. The box. Even now, her thoughts circled back to it, the dark weight of its presence lurking in the back of her mind.

She clutched her jacket tighter around herself, hoping the fabric would protect her from the cold, though the chill inside her felt far worse than the rain. She couldn't shake the feeling that something was following her, that eyes were watching her every step. She looked over her shoulder, half-expecting to see someone, anyone, trailing just out of sight. But the street was empty, save for the distant hum of traffic and the occasional shadow moving beneath the streetlights. There was no one there. But that didn't make her feel any safer.

As she walked aimlessly, her mind replayed the words in the book over and over again. They are watching. They always have been. The simple, chilling sentence had burned itself into her thoughts. Who were they? Who had written those words? And why now? Why had they been waiting for her?

She stopped in front of a small café. The windows were fogged up from the warmth inside, and for a moment, she considered going in. Maybe a cup of coffee would help calm her nerves. Maybe it would give her a moment to think, to figure out what to do next. But something about the quiet inside, the stillness, made her hesitate. It felt wrong. Almost like walking into a trap. She turned away from the café and kept walking, her pace quickening, though she wasn't sure where she was headed. The street seemed endless, stretching out in all directions, yet she felt like she was getting nowhere.

Her phone buzzed suddenly, a sharp, intrusive sound that made her jump. She fumbled for it, her hands slick with sweat, and looked at the screen.

A single text message from an unknown number.

"You're not alone. Don't trust anyone."

Her heart skipped a beat. Her fingers hovered over the screen, unsure of what to do. Who had sent this? The words felt urgent, but how could she trust them? How could she trust anything, anyone, right now?

She glanced around the empty street again, her pulse hammering in her throat. Was someone watching her? Was this a warning, or just another cruel mind game? She quickly deleted the message, but the paranoia lingered, gnawing at her from the inside.

She reached a crosswalk and paused at the corner, waiting for the light to change. As she stood there, she couldn't shake the feeling that something was off. The streets were quiet, almost too quiet. No honking horns, no chatter from passing pedestrians, no distant sirens. It was as though the entire city had fallen silent, just waiting. Watching.

Then, the sound of footsteps reached her ears. Slow, deliberate steps, echoing in the stillness of the night. Lily turned, her heart thumping as she scanned the empty sidewalk. Nothing. There was no one there. The street was deserted.

She frowned, feeling a wave of unease wash over her. She'd heard those footsteps—clearly heard them. The sounds of shoes against pavement, the unmistakable rhythm of someone walking toward her. But when she turned around, there was nothing. No one.

The light changed, and she crossed the street quickly, her mind spinning with questions she couldn't answer. She didn't want to look over her shoulder again. She didn't want to feel like she was being hunted. But she had to. She couldn't ignore it.

Her eyes scanned the darkness behind her, and just as her breath caught in her throat, she saw him.

A man stood at the far end of the street, his figure partially obscured by a streetlamp. He was tall, his silhouette shadowed in the dim light, but there was something about him that made her blood run cold. He wasn't moving. He was just standing there, watching her. And the worst part was, she had no idea how long he had been there. She hadn't heard him approach.

She stopped walking, her legs suddenly feeling like they might give way. The man's gaze seemed to pierce through the distance, locking onto her with a chilling intensity. She wanted to look away, to run, but her body wouldn't respond. It was as though some invisible force was holding her in place, forcing her to meet his gaze.

Then, without warning, the man turned and walked away. The sound of his footsteps receded into the night, fading until it was nothing more than a faint echo.

Lily's breath came in ragged gasps, her body trembling with fear. What was that? Was he real? Was he another hallucination brought on by the stress and terror of everything that had been happening to her? Or was he something more? A part of whatever twisted game she had been thrown into?

She shook her head, trying to steady herself. She couldn't afford to lose it now. She had to keep going. She had to find answers. But what if this was all part of something bigger? What if the people behind all of this were already here, in the city, watching her every move?

Suddenly, the phone buzzed again. Her pulse spiked. She pulled it from her pocket, her hands shaking as she glanced at the screen. Another message, this time with an unfamiliar number.

"It's happening. Be ready."

Her stomach churned. Who was sending these messages? Were they related to the box? To the man who had been watching her? She felt trapped, isolated, as if every move she made was being orchestrated by someone else. She couldn't trust the messages, she knew that. But she also couldn't ignore them. They were too precise, too eerily timed.

Before she could think any more about it, her phone buzzed yet again.

"Look behind you."

The blood drained from Lily's face. Her heart skipped a beat, and she froze in place, unable to move. Her hand was still clutching the phone, her fingers numb with cold sweat.

Look behind you.

Her head snapped around involuntarily, her eyes scanning the street in every direction. But there was no one. The street was still empty. The rain had picked up again, a fine mist settling in the air. But there was no sign of the man, no sign of anyone following her. Nothing. Just the empty, hollow street stretching out before her.

She swallowed hard, forcing her breath to calm. It was just a prank. It had to be. Some sick joke played on her by whoever was behind all this. But she couldn't shake the feeling that something was wrong. Something was out of place. And as much as she wanted to deny it, she couldn't help but feel that she was being led somewhere, drawn into a trap she couldn't escape.

Suddenly, a loud, piercing sound cut through the night, a siren wailing in the distance. Lily flinched, her heart racing as the wail grew louder. It sounded close. Too close.

The siren stopped abruptly.

The silence that followed was more deafening than the wail of the siren. It was like the city had swallowed the sound, leaving only the pounding of her own heart in her ears.

And then, there was a knock.

Soft at first, as though coming from behind a door, then louder, more insistent. The knock echoed in her mind, matching the rhythm of the siren's wail. It seemed to come from all around her, surrounding her, trapping her in the sound. She looked around, her pulse skyrocketing, her breath ragged.

It wasn't a coincidence. Whatever was happening, it was happening now.

And Lily was running out of time.

25

The untouched Box

The box sat on the kitchen counter, the brown cardboard edges curled slightly from where it had been sealed, its mysterious contents hidden beneath the simple, nondescript packaging. Lily hadn't touched it since the moment it arrived. She had been too afraid to, too cautious, but the longer she stared at it, the more it gnawed at her. There was something she needed to know. Something that would make sense of everything—the messages, the phone calls, the strange man who had appeared from nowhere. She had to open it. She had to understand.

She glanced around the room, her heartbeat thudding in her chest. The quiet was deafening. The apartment, once a place of refuge, now felt like a cage. Every creak of the floorboards, every soft rustle from the other side of the thin walls seemed magnified. She felt eyes on her, the unmistakable sensation of being watched, even though she knew she was alone. Or was she?

Lily shook her head, trying to banish the paranoia that threatened to consume her. She was losing herself in the uncertainty, allowing fear to cloud her judgment. No. She had to be strong. She had to face this. The box was the key to everything.

She reached for it, her fingers trembling as they brushed against the rough surface of the cardboard. The weight of it seemed wrong, somehow. Heavier than it should have been for something so small. She picked it up carefully, her hands shaking from a mixture of anxiety and something else— something far more primal, more insistent.

With a deep breath, she set it down on the dining table. The dim light of the apartment flickered overhead as she took a step back, inspecting the box once more. There was no return address. No name. Nothing to indicate where it had come from or why it had been sent to her. It was as though the box had appeared out of thin air, dropped onto her doorstep without explanation.

Her fingers grazed the edge of the tape, and she paused, suddenly overcome by the irrational fear that whatever was inside would change everything. She didn't know what it was. She didn't know if she was ready to know. But there was no going back now.

With a sharp motion, she tore through the tape, the sound of it slicing through the air making her jump. The box resisted for a moment, and then gave way, its contents spilling out onto the table in a flurry of motion.

Lily recoiled, her breath catching in her throat.

Inside the box was a stack of old photographs. A dozen or more, each one worn at the edges, yellowed with age. The images were blurred, the faces barely discernible, but there was something deeply familiar about them. She picked one up, turning it over in her hands, as if waiting for something to make sense. There was a sense of coldness that washed over her as she recognized the location. It was a street she knew—one she had walked down countless times as a child. But what chilled her the most wasn't the street—it was the people in the photo.

They were standing on that very same street, their faces frozen in time, staring directly at the camera. It was a family, she realized. Her family. But there was something wrong with the image. Something subtle. The people were blurred, their features indistinct, their eyes... too dark, too empty. The photograph looked almost as if it had been altered—distorted in some way, as if someone had taken great care to erase their humanity.

Her hands shook as she set the photograph down, trying to steady herself. She didn't know why, but this photo—the family photo—made her stomach twist. She had never seen it before. She didn't recognize the other faces, even though she knew they should be familiar. But something about the emptiness in their eyes, the distortion of their features... it was as though they weren't people at all. Not real. Not her family.

With a trembling breath, she picked up another photograph. This one was different. It showed a young girl sitting alone in a dark room, her face partially hidden by a curtain. But the thing that made her stomach drop wasn't the girl's expression—it was the fact that the girl looked exactly like Lily. Same long brown hair, same pale skin, same eyes. The only difference was the subtle distortion of the image, the way the girl's face seemed to shift ever so slightly. It was as if the photograph was trying to tell her something, trying to show her something she wasn't meant to see.

Lily slammed the photos back into the box, her hands trembling uncontrollably now. She could feel the sweat building on her skin, the air in the room growing heavier. The box, the photographs—they were all a part of this twisted game. But what was the game? What did it all mean?

Her phone buzzed, the sudden sound startling her. She jerked her head toward the screen, half-expecting it to be another cryptic message, another warning, but when she saw the sender's name, her breath caught.

It was from her mother.

Lily hesitated for a moment, her fingers frozen over the screen. Her mother hadn't contacted her in months—not since everything had started to fall apart. Not since the day Lily had moved into the apartment. Since then, the only connection she had with her family was the distant, unsettling feeling that had followed her from place to place. She had tried calling her mother—tried reaching out for answers—but there was never a response.

Now, here was the message. She opened it with shaking hands.

"They're coming for you. Don't trust the box. Get out of the apartment."

Her breath caught in her throat, her pulse skyrocketing. The words swam before her eyes as her mind raced, trying to make sense of it. Her mother knew. She knew something. What was happening? Who was coming for her?

Lily's heart pounded in her chest as she looked down at the box, its contents still spilling out across the table. Her mind whirled. She had been so focused on the photographs, so desperate to understand, that she hadn't thought about the danger. What if everything that had been happening—the phone calls, the cryptic messages, the box itself—was part of something far more sinister than she could comprehend?

She stood up abruptly, the chair scraping loudly against the floor as she backed away from the table. Her breath was shallow, and the room seemed to close in on her, the walls pressing against her chest. She was suffocating. She needed to leave. She needed to get out of the apartment before it was too late.

Without thinking, she grabbed her jacket and shoved her phone into her pocket, darting toward the door. She didn't even stop to grab her purse. She didn't care about anything anymore—she just needed to get away. But as she reached for the doorknob, she froze.

There, just beyond the doorframe, stood a figure.

It was the man—the one who had been following her, watching

her. His face was obscured by shadows, but she could see the outline of his form, the way he stood, still as a statue.

Her heart pounded painfully in her chest, a cold sweat breaking out across her forehead.

"Don't open it," the man's voice came, low and gravelly. "You don't know what you're dealing with."

Lily's breath caught in her throat. There was nowhere to run now. No escape.

26

The False Alarm

Lily's breath was shallow, the air thick with the weight of dread as she stood motionless in the doorway, her fingers frozen around the cold metal doorknob. The figure before her—tall, shadowed, silent—loomed like a dark presence, filling the narrow hallway with an almost suffocating aura. He hadn't moved. Neither had she. The seconds stretched, thick and taut, like the moment before a thunderstorm breaks.

"Who are you?" Lily's voice was barely a whisper, a tremor escaping her lips. She had prepared herself for many things, but not for this. Not for a man standing at her door, in her home, uninvited and unknown.

The man didn't answer right away. His face was obscured by shadows, his features indistinct, but his presence was undeniable. There was something unsettling about him, a stillness that made the air around them seem to hold its breath.

"I warned you," he said, his voice raspy, yet eerily calm. "The box—it's a trap. You shouldn't have opened it."

Lily's pulse quickened. His words struck her with the force of a sudden jolt. He knew about the box. He knew everything. But who was he? And why was he warning her now? She felt the unsettling sensation again, as though someone had been watching her every move from the shadows, tracking her every breath.

"I don't understand," she stammered, trying to keep her composure. "What do you want from me? Why are you here?"

The man took a step forward, and Lily instinctively recoiled, her back pressing against the doorframe. Her mind raced, thoughts swirling in an incoherent mess. Was he here to hurt her? To finish what had started? Or was this just another part of the twisted puzzle she had been trying so desperately to solve?

"I'm not here to hurt you," the man said, his voice softening just slightly. "But you're in danger. You've opened something you shouldn't have. Now they know."

"Who?" Lily's mind screamed, the question tumbling from her lips before she could stop it. "Who knows? What's going to happen?"

The man's eyes—if they could even be called eyes—glinted in the dim light, dark as pitch. He seemed to study her for a long moment before he spoke again, his words deliberate and heavy with meaning.

"The people who sent that box aren't just playing games. They'll come for you. They'll come for you because they've marked you, Lily. You've seen too much."

Lily swallowed hard. His words hit her like a slap. Marked her? Seen too much? Was she a part of something she didn't even understand? She wasn't sure she could comprehend it all. She wasn't sure she wanted to. But one thing was clear: the terror she had been feeling for days—weeks, even—was no accident. It wasn't just paranoia. Something was happening, something far worse than she had imagined.

"Why are you telling me this?" Her voice cracked. She wasn't sure if she was ready to hear the answer.

The man hesitated, as though weighing the decision in his mind. Finally, he took another step closer, and Lily instinctively pushed herself against the door, her heart racing. She could feel the presence of the man's nearness like a physical force, pressing in from all sides.

"Because you're the key," he said, his voice low and urgent. "And they're going to find you. They're going to come after you. You've opened Pandora's box."

Lily's stomach twisted into a knot. She tried to steady herself, tried to focus on his words, but it was impossible. Nothing about this made sense. She wasn't anyone special. She was just a woman, living alone in an apartment, trying to move on from the chaos of her past. But the more she thought about the box, the photographs, the strange man in front of her, the more the pieces seemed to fit into a puzzle she hadn't yet solved.

"I don't know what you mean," she whispered, shaking her head as if trying to deny it all. "I don't know what's happening. I don't know who you are."

"You will," the man said, his voice sharp now, a dangerous edge creeping in. "But it will be too late by then."

Lily was frozen, trapped in the moment. It was as if time had slowed, each heartbeat loud in her ears, as though she could feel her life unraveling in front of her. She wanted to run. She wanted to scream, to make the man disappear, but every part of her body seemed paralyzed. Her instincts told her to act, but her mind was telling her to be cautious. She had to get answers. She had to understand before it was too late.

"What happens now?" she asked, her voice trembling. "What do I do?"

The man's eyes flickered toward the hallway, as though sensing something. Then, in a voice that was almost too quiet to hear, he said, "It's too late to escape. The trap has already been set."

Lily's heart skipped a beat. The words echoed in her head. The trap had been set. What did he mean? How could she possibly escape something she didn't even understand?

Before she could ask another question, the man's posture shifted. His body tensed, like a predator sensing prey nearby, his head jerking toward the hallway.

Lily's blood ran cold. She turned her head sharply, the feeling of being watched now impossible to ignore. The temperature in the room seemed to drop suddenly, as if the very air had turned stale and thick. The oppressive silence of the apartment was broken only by the faint sound of a distant thudding—a slow, deliberate rhythm, as if something was drawing nearer.

Footsteps.

Lily's breath hitched as she watched the man's eyes dart toward her, a warning flashing across his face. "They're here."

"What?" Her voice was barely audible as panic began to claw its way up her throat. "Who's here? Who's coming?"

"Get out," the man hissed, his voice urgent, nearly frantic now. "Now."

Lily's hands were shaking as she backed away from the door, but the figure in front of her stepped forward with surprising speed, blocking her path. "You can't leave through the door," he said quickly. "They'll be waiting for you."

Lily's mind spun. What was happening? Who was this man? What did he mean by "they"? And how did he know about the danger she was in?

He grabbed her wrist, pulling her toward the back of the apartment, his grip surprisingly strong. She tried to pull away, but his hold tightened, and she realized that if she didn't follow, she might not have any chance of escape. She didn't know who to trust—him, or the unknown force threatening her—but right now, she had no choice. She had to move.

"Stay quiet," he warned, his breath coming in sharp, heavy gasps. "If you want to survive this, you have to trust me."

Lily didn't answer. She couldn't. Her heart pounded in her chest as she was pulled through the apartment, the sound of footsteps growing louder. She didn't know who was chasing her. She didn't know who the man was. But one thing was certain: time had run out.

The trap had been set. And there was no way to undo it.

27

The Unopened Box

Lily's heart raced as she stepped cautiously through the darkened apartment, the air thick with tension. The man's grip on her wrist was firm, his fingers like iron, his presence imposing and immediate. She tried to pull away, but the urgency in his eyes made her freeze. She didn't know who he was, or what he wanted, but there was something about him—something deep and unsettling—that made her feel like she had no choice but to follow.

The distant sound of footsteps grew louder, echoing through the empty halls. There was no mistaking it now; whoever was coming for them was getting closer. And the man, the one who had warned her, had no intention of letting her face whatever was out there alone.

"Do you trust me?" he asked, his voice harsh, almost a whisper.

Lily opened her mouth, but the words wouldn't come. Did she trust him? No. Every fiber of her being screamed that he was dangerous, but there was something more pressing right now. The trap he'd spoken about—whatever it was—was closing in, and she had to do something. There was no time to ask questions, to figure things out. She had to move.

She nodded.

He didn't wait for more. Without a word, he yanked her along, through the living room, past the broken furniture and shattered glass from the previous night's chaos. He didn't seem to notice the mess; his eyes were trained forward, as though he could see something she couldn't, something lurking in the shadows.

Lily's mind whirled. Everything was spiraling out of control. Her life had been turned upside down the moment she received that damned box. She couldn't even remember when it had arrived, only the chill that had seeped into her bones when she first laid eyes on it. It had sat there on the kitchen counter, unopened, for days. It wasn't until she had received the ominous warning from the unknown sender that she'd finally dared to open it. And then, the photographs. The strange symbols. The message.

It wasn't just a warning; it was a countdown.

The man pulled her into the hallway, his pace quickening as they approached the back of the apartment, a part she hadn't paid much attention to before. The bedroom, the bathroom, a tiny closet that seemed too small to even be useful—it was all empty now. But there was one place she hadn't thought to check. One place that had stood out ever since she moved in.

The closet under the stairs.

A faint light flickered from the small space at the far end of the hall. It cast long, eerie shadows against the walls, and the closer they got, the more Lily's skin prickled with fear. The man didn't speak as he led her to it, but Lily could see the tension in his shoulders, the way his eyes darted toward the door with a sense of urgency.

He stopped just in front of it, his hand tightening around the knob.

"This is it," he said, his voice barely audible. "Inside. Now."

Lily hesitated for only a moment before she moved toward him, her breath quickening. She wasn't sure what was going to happen, but she knew she didn't have a choice. She had to go in.

The man flung the door open with a loud creak. The space beyond was dark and cramped, the kind of space people usually hid things they didn't want others to see. And in the farthest corner, hidden behind a stack of old boxes and furniture, was something that caught her eye.

A chest.

It was made of dark wood, ancient-looking, covered in layers of dust. The brass hinges were tarnished, but the lock gleamed in the faint light. It was the kind of chest that screamed mystery—secrets locked inside, too dangerous to be let out. She felt an instinctive chill crawl up her spine. Was this the box the man had been warning her about? Was this the one?

"You have to open it," the man urged, his voice rough. "It's the only way."

She turned to him, her heart hammering. "What is it? What's inside?"

"You don't want to know," he said darkly, his eyes locking with hers. "But you need to. It's your only chance."

Her breath caught in her throat. Lily took a shaky step forward, her hand trembling as she reached for the chest. The lock clicked as she turned the rusted key, the sound sharp in the silence, and the lid creaked open slowly.

Inside, there was nothing but darkness. A black void that seemed to suck the light out of the room. She blinked, trying to focus, but it was impossible. It felt like the air itself was warping, thick and heavy, pressing against her chest.

And then she saw it.

At the bottom of the chest, nestled in dark velvet, was a single sheet of paper. It wasn't folded, just laid flat as though it had been waiting for her all this time. She reached for it, her fingers brushing the edges of the page, and felt a strange coldness seep into her skin. She pulled it out, unfolding it with trembling hands.

The message was simple, written in a clean, precise script.

"You've opened it. Now you must finish it."

Lily's stomach lurched. Finish it? Finish what?

She looked back at the man, his face hard, unreadable. His eyes were locked on the paper, and he stepped closer, his voice low.

"It's a game," he said. "But not the kind you think. You've already played your part. Now, it's time for the rest of it."

Lily's mind raced. She didn't understand. What was happening? What game was he talking about? The countdown had already started. Hadn't it? The box, the message, the photographs—they all pointed toward something, some unknown conclusion that she couldn't decipher.

But now, standing in the shadowy corner of the apartment, she felt the weight of the words sink in. The message was more than just a warning. It was a command. She had opened something—something that wasn't meant to be disturbed—and now the consequences were playing out, right in front of her.

A loud bang echoed from the hallway, and Lily's body tensed. Her heart seemed to skip a beat as she turned toward the noise. Footsteps, sharp and deliberate, grew closer.

"They're here," the man hissed. "We have to go. Now."

Lily felt a surge of panic. She hadn't even processed what was happening, and now everything was spiraling out of control. The chest, the warning, the game—it was all connected, and she was standing at the center of it, unable to break free.

The man grabbed her arm once again, pulling her out of the small room. He was leading her toward the back door, his pace frantic now, his steps echoing in the narrow hallway.

"We're almost out of time," he muttered under his breath, glancing over his shoulder. "They know you're here. They've been tracking you."

Lily's chest tightened with a fresh wave of fear. "Who? Who's tracking me?"

The man didn't answer. He didn't need to. It was clear now. Whoever they were, they were closing in. The box had been a signal. A trigger. A countdown. And now, it was time to face whatever it had set in motion.

She didn't have time to ask more questions. The man flung open the door to the alleyway, and they were swallowed by the night. The cool air felt like a slap to her skin, but it did nothing to calm the storm brewing inside her. What was coming? What was she meant to finish?

And, most haunting of all: Was she already too late?

28

The wavering

Lena couldn't shake the feeling that something wasn't right. The old wooden door creaked as she stepped into the empty house, her heart thumping in her chest. The space was eerily quiet—too quiet. The kind of silence that hung heavily in the air, as if waiting for something to happen.

She glanced back over her shoulder, half-expecting someone to be standing behind her, but there was nothing. Just the overgrown yard, the tall trees swaying slightly in the wind. Still, she couldn't help but feel a deep unease as she moved further into the house, her footsteps echoing in the vast, empty space.

The message had been simple enough. A phone call late at night, the voice of a stranger on the other end. "You need to come. It's happening again."

Lena had been hesitant, sure it was some kind of prank, but the urgency in the voice had shaken her. And then there was the address—a place she knew well. The old house on the edge of town. She hadn't been there in years. The memories flooded back in an instant: the laughter of her childhood, the smell of fresh cookies baking in the kitchen, the warmth of family. But now, as she stood in the doorway, those memories felt distant and hollow, swallowed by the weight of the present.

The silence pressed against her, the air thick with tension. She moved through the house, the wooden floors groaning under her weight. There was no sign of anyone, no sign of anything out of the ordinary. Just the dust settling in the corners, the faint scent of mildew hanging in the air. But something didn't sit right.

The phone call had seemed so real, so urgent. The voice had sounded desperate, frantic even. And the more Lena thought about it, the more she realized how familiar the tone had been. She couldn't quite place it, but there was something about it that felt like a memory, a shadow lurking just beyond her reach. But who would have called her? Who would have known to send her here? It didn't make sense.

The floorboards creaked ahead of her as she stepped cautiously into the living room. The heavy curtains were drawn, casting long, dark shadows that seemed to stretch toward her like fingers, reaching out to pull her into the unknown. She stood frozen in the doorway, her breath catching in her throat.

Suddenly, the phone rang again.

Lena jumped, the sudden noise jarring in the stillness of the house. She quickly pulled her phone from her pocket, her hand shaking slightly. The number on the screen was unfamiliar, but the same strange, urgent feeling stirred in her chest.

"Hello?" she answered, trying to steady her voice.

There was silence on the other end.

Lena frowned. "Hello? Who is this?"

The voice she heard next was low, barely a whisper. "It's happening again, Lena. You have to get out."

The hairs on the back of her neck stood on end. The voice was distorted, the words almost indecipherable, but the message was clear. Someone knew something. Someone was watching her, and they had somehow connected her to whatever this was.

"Get out? Get out of where?" she asked, her pulse quickening.

"Lena... the house. It's coming for you. It knows you're here."

The line went dead.

Lena stood there for a moment, her heart pounding in her chest. Her mind raced, trying to make sense of the words, the tone, the urgency. She had to leave. But leave what? The house? Or was it something else entirely? The house had always been a place of comfort for her. Sure, it was old and creaky, but nothing had ever happened there that warranted fear.

Or had it?

A chill ran down her spine as memories of her childhood came flooding back. The house wasn't just a house. It was a place full of secrets, whispers that had never fully made sense. Her parents had always warned her not to go into the attic, to stay away from the old study room where the strange symbols had been carved into the walls. But she had never understood why. Now, as an adult, those warnings seemed more cryptic than ever.

Lena shook her head, trying to clear the thoughts from her mind. She needed to focus. She needed to figure out what was going on.

She moved toward the stairs, her feet dragging as if the weight of the house was pushing her down, pulling her deeper into something she didn't understand. The staircase groaned beneath her, each step a reminder of the years the house had stood undisturbed, each board creaking with age and neglect. The phone call had been a warning, but what was it warning her about?

At the top of the stairs, Lena paused. The long hallway stretched out before her, each door closed, the darkness within each room seeming to beckon her. She moved toward the door at the end of the hall, the one that had always been off-limits to her growing up. The study.

Her hand trembled as she reached for the doorknob. The air around her seemed to thicken, the temperature dropping, the silence swallowing her whole. She opened the door, the old hinges protesting loudly as she stepped inside. The room was exactly as she remembered it: dusty, filled with the scent of old books and stale air. A single window was cracked open, letting in a sliver of moonlight that illuminated the room in an eerie, pale glow.

And there, in the center of the room, was the desk. The one that had always frightened her as a child. The one her parents had kept locked. The one she had never dared to approach.

Now, the drawer was ajar.

Lena's heart skipped a beat. She approached the desk slowly, her breath shallow as she pulled open the drawer. Inside was a small, leather-bound book. She recognized it immediately. It was her father's journal—the one she had never been allowed to touch.

She flipped it open to the first page, her eyes scanning the faded handwriting.

"The house is calling. It's always been calling. It waits for the right time to awaken, and when it does, we must be ready."

Lena's fingers froze on the page. What was this? What had her father been writing about? She flipped through the pages quickly, scanning the disjointed entries. They spoke of strange dreams, of the house coming alive at night, of things moving in the shadows, of a darkness that had followed her family for generations.

The more she read, the more unsettled she became. Her father had known something. He had been preparing for something. Something that had to do with this house. The very house that had been her childhood home. The very house that now felt like a trap.

Suddenly, a loud crash from downstairs broke the stillness, snapping Lena out of her thoughts. Her head whipped around, her heart racing. What was that?

She dropped the journal and bolted toward the door, her feet stumbling as she rushed down the stairs. The house seemed to pulse with energy, the walls closing in around her, as if the entire structure was alive, watching her every move.

When she reached the living room, her eyes darted to the source of the noise. The window had shattered.

And there, standing in the doorway, was a figure.

Lena froze. The figure didn't move, didn't speak. But she could feel it. The weight of its presence. It was watching her. Waiting.

She took a cautious step back. "Who are you?"

The figure didn't respond. Instead, it stepped forward into the room, its form shrouded in darkness, barely visible in the dim light. Lena's breath caught in her throat. She had no idea who this person was, but the air around them was suffocating, heavy with something dangerous, something ancient.

"Lena..." The voice was soft, barely a whisper, but it sent a shiver down her spine. It was familiar, but distorted, like an echo from her past. "It's too late."

Her heart dropped.

Before she could react, the figure raised a hand, and the world around her seemed to tilt. The walls began to distort, twisting in impossible angles. The floor beneath her feet felt like it was shifting, becoming something she couldn't quite grasp.

And then, just as suddenly as it had started, everything went quiet.

Lena opened her eyes, but the figure was gone. The house was still. Silent once more.

But she knew, deep in her gut, that it hadn't been a false alarm. Something had changed. Something had awakened. And it was only a matter of time before it found her.

29

The Unexposed pack

The room smelled of dust and stale air, a musty scent that had long since settled into the very fabric of the house. Lena stood in the hallway, staring at the wooden door ahead of her, the one that had always been closed. The one that, for as long as she could remember, had been locked tight. It wasn't until the strange phone call—her mind flashing back to the disjointed warning—that she even thought to return to the house. Now, it seemed as if it was calling her back, pulling her in like a moth to a flame.

The house had been empty for years. Since her parents' death, she had never returned, not once, too many painful memories clinging to the walls, to the rooms where life had once been so full of laughter and love. But tonight, something had shifted. A message—cryptic, urgent—had drawn her here. And now, standing before the door, she realized that the feeling of dread that had been gnawing at her all evening was real. Whatever it was, it wasn't just in her head.

Lena's hand trembled as she reached for the brass doorknob. It was cold to the touch, far colder than it should have been, considering the warm summer night outside. The door creaked open with a groan that reverberated through the house, and she stepped inside, her senses instantly assaulted by the eerie stillness of the room.

The walls were lined with bookshelves, their contents heavy with the weight of years, and the small desk in the corner seemed untouched by time. But it was the box in the center of the room that caught her attention.

She froze.

It was sitting there, on the floor, covered in dust, as if it had been waiting for her. The box was small—no larger than a shoebox—and made of dark wood, polished and worn. The corners were rounded, and a thick leather strap wrapped tightly around it, keeping it closed. The faintest symbols were etched into the surface, the lines intricate and delicate, as though they had been carved by a hand that had known this box intimately.

A chill ran down Lena's spine.

For years, she had heard rumors of something hidden in this room. Something important, something that her parents had gone to great lengths to keep from her. She had never dared to investigate, to pry into the secrets that had been so carefully tucked away, but now the pull was undeniable. This box had to be part of it. It had to be.

She moved cautiously toward it, her breath catching in her throat. With every step, the air seemed to grow heavier, the silence suffocating. She could feel her heart pounding in her chest as she knelt down in front of the box, the floor creaking beneath her. The leather strap felt rough against her fingers as she slowly undid the clasp, the faintest sense of trepidation stirring in her gut.

It took every ounce of willpower not to hesitate, not to drop the strap and run, but she couldn't. Not now.

The clasp clicked open with an almost inaudible sound. Lena's breath caught, her pulse quickening as she slowly lifted the lid of the box.

Inside, nestled against a soft velvet lining, was an assortment of old papers and objects. The first thing that caught her eye was a yellowed envelope, its edges frayed and torn with age. The handwriting on the front was unmistakable.

Her father's.

Her hand trembled as she reached for the envelope. It was sealed with a crimson wax emblem, and the weight of it seemed far greater than it should have been. She could feel her stomach tighten as she broke the seal, slowly pulling the letter from its confines. The moment she opened it, the faint scent of her father's cologne, something she hadn't smelled in years, filled her nostrils. Her heart ached, but she pushed the emotion aside, focusing on the words written on the page.

"Lena,

"If you are reading this, then the time has come. The house is not what it seems. It never has been. You must understand that the thing in the house, the thing that you've always felt but never truly seen, is waiting. It is waking. And you—

"You are its key."

Lena's breath caught in her throat. She reread the letter, her eyes scanning the words in disbelief. The house... the thing in the house... What was he talking about? Her father had always been strange, distant in his later years, but this was something else entirely.

She pushed the letter aside, feeling a rising sense of panic as she reached for the other objects in the box. There were photographs—old ones, black and white—of her parents in younger days, standing together in front of the house, smiling, laughing. But the smiles on their faces didn't match the unease in their eyes. She recognized her father in every photograph, but it was her mother's face that seemed different, older somehow, as if time had taken a toll on her far more quickly than Lena remembered.

Lena shoved the photographs aside, her hands shaking as she pulled out the next item—a small, ornate key. The metal glinted in the dim light, and the intricate patterns etched into its surface seemed familiar, though she couldn't place where she had seen it before. She held it in her palm, the weight of it a strange comfort. What did it unlock?

And then there was a small, leather-bound journal—her father's handwriting again, but this time the words were hastily scrawled, as though he had been in a hurry.

"They're coming for you. I don't know how much time we have left. They know you're the one. Whatever happens, you must never go into the basement. Never. The door is locked for a reason."

Lena's chest tightened as she read the words. The basement. The one place she had always been warned never to go. It had always been locked, even when she was a child. But what was down there? What was so dangerous that her father had gone to such lengths to keep it hidden from her?

As she closed the journal, something else caught her eye—another photograph. This one, however, was not from the past. It was recent. A picture of her parents standing in front of the house, their faces obscured by shadows. And standing beside them, a figure Lena didn't recognize. A man. A tall man, dressed in black, his face hidden beneath the brim of a hat. His presence in the photograph sent a shiver through Lena, and she immediately flipped it over, hoping for an explanation.

The back was covered in scribbled words, her father's handwriting once again.

"He knows. He's the one who is coming for you."

Lena felt her breath catch in her throat. This wasn't just about the house anymore. This was something far more dangerous.

She had been drawn here for a reason, and whatever was waiting in the basement—whatever her father had been trying to protect her from—was closer than she realized.

Her eyes darted around the room, panic seizing her chest. It was impossible to ignore the growing feeling that the house was no longer just a house. It was something else entirely, something alive. And whatever it was, it had been waiting for her.

Lena slammed the box shut, the force of it echoing through the room. She stood up, her head spinning, the weight of the journal and the photographs pressing down on her, the key still cold in her hand. She had to leave. She had to get out of the house.

But as she turned to leave the room, the air shifted. The temperature dropped suddenly, and the door slammed shut behind her with a deafening bang.

Lena spun around, her heart racing, her breath coming in shallow gasps. And that was when she heard it. The unmistakable sound of footsteps.

Someone was in the house.

And they were coming for her.

30

The disappearing Witness

The cold seeping through the cracks of the old house was unbearable. Lena's breath came out in sharp, panicked bursts as she stood frozen in the middle of the hallway, the box still clutched tightly in her hands. Her mind raced, her pulse pounding in her ears. She had heard the footsteps—steady, deliberate—coming closer. They weren't a figment of her imagination. They were real. Someone was in the house with her.

The thought of being trapped in this place again, surrounded by memories and the twisted sense of danger that seemed to pulse through the very walls, made her stomach churn. Her parents were gone, but whoever—or whatever—was lurking in the shadows of this house was very much alive. And it had found her.

She glanced desperately at the nearest door. The study. She could make it there, lock herself in, and perhaps figure out what was going on. Maybe the answers she had uncovered in the box—the photographs, the journal, the key—would finally make sense. Maybe she could decipher her father's warnings before it was too late.

But before she could move, the sound of the footsteps grew louder. Closer. Someone was coming down the hallway.

Lena's heart skipped a beat. She instinctively stepped backward, her breath quickening. The footsteps had stopped. But she could still feel the presence in the air, as if the very floor beneath her was pressing down, urging her to run. The house seemed to close in on her, the walls pressing tighter, the silence thick and oppressive.

She stood there for a moment, her back pressed against the cold wood of the door. Her fingers clenched around the handle of the box, the symbols on the side of it now seeming to glow faintly in the dim light. What was in that basement? What had her father been trying to protect her from?

The footsteps started again, slow, almost deliberate. They were unmistakably heavy now, echoing against the wooden floor. It was clear that the intruder was moving toward her, not in a rush, but with purpose, as if they were certain she had nowhere to go.

Lena glanced down at the box, then to the hallway. If she could just make it out the back door, maybe she could escape. She didn't have time to process everything—the answers, the truth—she just needed to get out.

Her hand reached for the doorknob of the study, but before she could turn it, the door at the end of the hallway creaked open. The figure stood there in the shadows, partially obscured by the dim light from the hallway.

Lena froze.

It was a man. Tall, his features shrouded in the gloom, only his silhouette visible. He didn't speak, didn't move, just stood there, watching her.

She felt the weight of his gaze pressing down on her chest. Something in her gut told her to run, to escape before he had the chance to do whatever he had come to do. But she couldn't move. It was as if the air itself had become too thick to breathe, too heavy to lift her feet from the ground.

And then the voice came.

It was low, rasping, as if it had been stretched through years of disuse. The words were slow and deliberate.

"You've been looking in the wrong places, Lena."

Lena's body stiffened, the blood in her veins running cold. She didn't recognize the voice, but she had no doubt that it belonged to the man in front of her. Her mind scrambled for answers, memories flashing through her like a whirlwind. Had she seen him before? Heard his voice in passing? No. This man—he was someone new. Someone dangerous.

"Who are you?" Lena finally managed to force the words out, her voice trembling with a mix of fear and defiance.

The man didn't answer immediately. He took a single step forward, his eyes flickering to the box still clutched in her hands.

"You don't understand, do you?" His words dripped with something akin to pity, but there was no kindness in them. "Your father... he didn't protect you. Not really."

Lena felt her chest tighten, her breath coming faster. This couldn't be happening. Her father—he'd warned her. He had tried so hard to keep her away from this house, from whatever was hidden here. But why? Why hadn't he told her everything?

"I—" Lena's voice broke. "What do you want from me?"

The man took another slow, deliberate step toward her. The sound of his boots against the floorboard echoed in the silence, each one reverberating through the house like a death knell.

"I don't want anything from you, Lena," he said, his tone softening, almost coaxing. "I want you to understand. To see. To know the truth."

Lena shook her head, her stomach churning. This was too much. She couldn't take it. She had no idea what was going on, what this man wanted, or why everything was suddenly unraveling in front of her. Her father's cryptic warning, the box, the photographs, the key—it all felt like pieces of a puzzle that didn't fit together.

"No," she whispered, taking a step back. "I don't want to know."

But the man didn't relent. He took another step forward, this time more urgently, as if he knew she was about to slip away. He reached into the folds of his dark coat and pulled something out—an old, tattered photograph.

Lena's eyes widened as she took in the image. It was her. But it was a version of her she didn't recognize. She looked younger, far younger, her eyes wide with a look of terror. She was standing in front of the house, just like in the other photographs, but this time something was different. The figure standing next to her was not her father, not anyone she knew.

It was the man in front of her.

Lena staggered backward, her breath quickening, her heart pounding in her chest. "No... no. This isn't real. This can't be real."

The man's lips curled into a faint, almost sad smile. "It's as real as the house you're standing in. As real as the secrets you've tried so desperately to bury."

Her hands shook as she reached out for the photograph, but he pulled it away, holding it just out of her reach.

"Your parents made sure you would never remember," he said,

his voice growing more insistent, more pressing. "But now you must. The truth is more dangerous than you know, Lena. It's why they kept you away from here. It's why they hid the box. And it's why you're here now."

Lena's mind spun, trying to process what he was saying, but the words wouldn't settle. Her father had hidden things from her—things that were meant to be left forgotten. But why hadn't he told her? What had she done to deserve being kept in the dark for so long?

"Why are you telling me this?" she demanded, her voice cracking with desperation.

The man's smile widened. "Because you need to see it for yourself."

Without warning, he stepped aside, revealing a darkened doorway behind him. Lena's gaze flickered toward it, her breath catching in her throat. There, at the end of the hallway, was the entrance to the basement.

The door was ajar.

Lena's legs froze in place. She knew, deep down, that the answers she had been searching for—the truth about her parents, about this house, about herself—lay beyond that door. And yet, every instinct screamed at her to run, to turn away and never look back. But there was no escaping now. The door was open.

And so, with trembling hands, she took one step forward.

31

The Reappearing Object

The sound of the wind howling outside was the only thing that kept Lena from losing herself in the suffocating silence of the house. Every breath she took felt strained, like the air around her had thickened into something dense and impenetrable. The basement door stood open before her, like a dark mouth waiting to swallow her whole. But she didn't hesitate this time. Something—some invisible force—pulled her forward, urging her into the darkness.

The house creaked as she moved, the old floorboards groaning beneath her weight. She could almost feel the house's heartbeat, thumping against her chest, as though it was alive, aware of her every step. The corridor stretched out before her like a tunnel, the lights dim and flickering. The basement door loomed ahead, its edges dark and jagged like the mouth of some hungry beast.

Lena swallowed hard, the weight of the man's words still echoing in her ears. "The truth is more dangerous than you know." What was he talking about? What had her parents hidden? And why had he—whoever he was—come here now, to reveal it to her?

As she reached the door, her hand trembling, she paused. The air grew colder here, colder than the rest of the house, and the scent of mildew filled her nostrils. The basement felt like a place that had been left untouched for years. The darkness at the bottom of the stairs beckoned, and yet, she couldn't shake the feeling that something—or someone—was waiting for her.

She turned the handle. It creaked loudly, as though protesting the intrusion, but it gave way. The stairwell stretched downward into the gloom, the faintest hint of an eerie, musty smell rising from below.

She descended carefully, the sound of her shoes tapping softly on the wooden steps the only noise she could focus on. With each step, the air grew heavier, thicker. Her pulse raced in her ears, the adrenaline making her dizzy. What could be down there? What was her father hiding in this basement?

Halfway down, she froze. A flicker of movement caught her eye. A shadow, shifting just out of the corner of her vision. Her breath hitched as she squinted into the darkness below. There was something—someone—there.

But when she focused her eyes, there was nothing. The shadow disappeared.

"Get a grip," she muttered to herself, her voice sounding

strange and hollow in the confined space. "You're just imagining things."

Still, the hair on the back of her neck stood on end. The air felt
charged now, almost electric. The silence was broken only by
the faint hum of her own heartbeat, growing louder and louder
with each step she took down into the basement.

As she reached the bottom, the full extent of the basement
revealed itself. Dim light from a single, flickering bulb cast
long shadows against the stone walls. The room was vast,
stretching out before her like a cave, the far wall hidden in
shadow. Wooden crates and old furniture were scattered across
the floor, covered in dust, as though forgotten by time.

And then her eyes landed on something that made her stop dead
in her tracks.

There, in the far corner of the room, was a small wooden
box. It sat innocently atop an old, tattered rug. But there was
something about it that made her heart skip a beat. The same
box she had seen in the photographs. The one her father had
hidden. It was unmistakable.

Lena's hand shook as she reached out toward it, her pulse racing
in her throat. She knew what it was. She knew what she had to
do. And yet, as her fingers brushed against the smooth wood,
something within her screamed that she should stop. But she
couldn't.

The moment her fingers made contact with the box, a strange

sensation flooded through her—a jolt of cold that shot up her arm and made her skin crawl. She jerked back, her breath coming in short gasps.

Her heart pounded in her chest as she turned the box over. The symbols were still there, those strange markings that had appeared in her dreams. The same ones that had been in her father's journal. But there was something else, something she hadn't noticed before. A small latch, hidden beneath a layer of dust, glimmering faintly in the dim light.

With trembling hands, Lena slid the latch open.

The box opened with an eerie creak, and for a moment, Lena thought she saw something inside—a glimmer of silver, perhaps a key—but it was gone, swallowed by the darkness within the box. She blinked, staring into the interior, confused and unsettled.

Had she imagined it? She looked closer, but the box was empty. Nothing but dust and shadows.

Frustration twisted inside her. Had she come all this way for nothing? She was about to close the box, feeling the weight of disappointment settle over her, when she saw it.

A faint glimmer of light—a reflection—caught her eye.

She froze, her heart stuttering in her chest. The reflection was unmistakable, shimmering from the far corner of the basement, casting a brief, faint glow against the stone wall.

Lena turned toward it instinctively, her mind racing. What could it be? A mirror? A piece of glass?

Her eyes darted over the room, trying to pinpoint the source, but there was nothing obvious. No mirror. No glass. Just the shadowy clutter of old furniture and boxes. But the glimmer persisted, like a trick of the light.

Without thinking, she walked toward it, her footsteps echoing through the vast, empty basement. Her mind raced with possibilities. What could cause such a light? Was it something from the box? A hidden compartment? Or was it the house itself playing tricks on her?

As she neared the corner, the glimmer flickered again, only to disappear the moment her foot touched the ground. Lena's eyes widened.

It was gone.

She stood still for a moment, her breath catching in her throat. Had she imagined it? Or had something in the room caused that light to vanish so suddenly? She couldn't be sure. Her hands trembled as she looked around the corner.

There, nestled between two old crates, was a small, gleaming object. A key. A key that had not been there before.

Her heart skipped a beat. How could it have appeared so suddenly? She hadn't seen it when she had looked just moments ago.

With shaky hands, she bent down and picked it up. The metal was cold against her fingertips, its surface smooth and worn with age. But there was no mistaking it. This was the key. The one she had seen in the photographs, the one her father had hidden.

The air in the room felt colder now, heavier, as though the walls themselves were closing in. The basement had become a prison, a trap, and she had walked right into it.

Lena stood up slowly, turning the key over in her hands. A thousand questions filled her mind. Where did this key lead? And why had it appeared when it had? Was it connected to the mystery of the house? Of her parents?

Before she could take another step, she heard it.

A faint whisper, just beyond the range of hearing. A voice, so soft and distant, that it could have been a figment of her imagination.

But she heard it again.

"Lena..."

She spun around, her heart leaping in her chest, but there was no one there. The room remained as still and silent as ever.

And yet, in that moment, Lena knew.

She had just uncovered the first piece of a puzzle that had been waiting for her. A puzzle that would lead her deeper into the darkness of this house, into the secrets that had been hidden from her for so long.

The key was the answer.

And now, she had no choice but to follow its path.

32

The Witness

Lena stood frozen, her pulse thumping in her ears. The key, so small and unassuming in her palm, seemed to burn against her skin. It felt as though it was alive, thrumming with an energy she couldn't explain. Her fingers clenched around it involuntarily, and for a moment, she wondered if it would break her skin. But the key remained solid, unyielding, a symbol of something far darker than she could yet comprehend.

She glanced around the basement once more, the shadows stretching long across the stone walls, the flickering light above casting ominous shapes on the floor. The whisper—her name, soft as a breath, barely there—still echoed in her mind. She turned slowly, scanning the dimly lit space as if expecting to find someone standing there, watching her. But the basement was empty. The silence had returned, pressing down on her chest like a weight.

Her breath came in shallow bursts. She had to move. But where? The air was thick, and every step felt like it was weighted with the secrets of the house. She hadn't meant to end up here. She hadn't meant to unearth the mysteries buried so deep within the walls of her parents' home. But there was no turning back now.

Clutching the key tightly, Lena backed away from the corner where she had found it. Her footsteps echoed on the hard, cold floor, too loud in the quiet. She could feel something in the room shift, a sense of being watched, though there was no one there. She turned quickly, scanning the shadows, but still, nothing.

Her mind raced. Who was the man in the photographs? Why had he appeared when she opened the box? And most importantly—what did the key unlock?

The thought of venturing further into the house made her stomach churn. The walls felt like they were closing in around her, each step she took echoing louder than the last. Every room she entered seemed to hold more questions than answers. And every time she thought she was getting closer to the truth, something—some strange force—seemed to pull her back.

The silence of the basement felt almost oppressive now. The air seemed too still, too thick. It pressed against her skin, as though it were holding something back. She couldn't shake the feeling that she was missing something. Something just out of her reach.

A creak broke the silence. A sound so faint, so subtle, that she almost didn't hear it at first. But then it came again, sharper this time, echoing through the basement like a door opening. A door that had been locked for years, perhaps. The sound was faint but unmistakable, like a footstep on the creaky wooden stairs above.

Lena's heart skipped a beat. She wasn't alone.

Her hand instinctively went to the pocket of her jacket, where she kept her phone, but it wasn't there. Panic flooded her chest. She had left it upstairs. Alone in the basement, with no way to call for help, no way to communicate with anyone. She had never felt more isolated, more vulnerable.

The sound came again, closer this time. A slow, deliberate footstep. She strained to hear, her body tense, every muscle on edge. She couldn't tell where it was coming from. It could have been above her, behind her—she didn't know. All she knew was that it was getting closer. And she was trapped.

A sudden flicker of light above her head startled her, and she looked up just in time to see the bulb sputter and die. The basement was plunged into darkness. Her breath hitched, and she reached out instinctively, groping for anything to steady herself against. Her fingers brushed the cold, rough surface of the wall, and she pressed her back against it, her breath coming in shallow gasps.

The silence that followed felt suffocating. The darkness around her seemed to close in, oppressive and thick. Lena's heartbeat pounded in her throat. Every sound, every creak of the house felt amplified, as though it were all happening inside her mind.

And then—another noise.

This time, it was unmistakable.

A voice.

"Lena..."

The whisper came from somewhere in the dark, distant but clear. It was not a man's voice, though. It was softer, more familiar—like a woman's voice. It sounded like... her mother's.

Lena froze. She couldn't breathe. The air seemed to leave her lungs, replaced by a tight, unbearable pressure. Her mother's voice. But that was impossible. Her mother had been gone for years.

The voice called again, this time louder, more insistent. "Lena... help me."

Lena's mind raced. Her mother had died long before she could remember. How could this be? Was it just her imagination? Or was it something else? Something that had been waiting for her all these years?

She felt a shiver crawl up her spine. The air around her seemed to crackle, as though the very fabric of reality had been torn open, leaving a doorway into something darker. She couldn't stay here. She couldn't wait to find out what was going on. She had to get out, back to safety.

But as she turned to leave, something caught her eye. A movement in the darkness. The faintest outline of a figure. At first, she thought it was just her mind playing tricks on her, the shadows blending together to form a shape. But the figure didn't move like the shadows. It was too real.

Lena froze. The figure was tall, its edges blurred, as if it were standing just outside the reach of the light. She could see its features—pale skin, hollow eyes, and a mouth that was open as if it were about to speak. But no sound came. The figure just stood there, staring at her with unblinking eyes.

"Who... who are you?" Lena whispered, her voice trembling.

The figure didn't respond. Instead, it took a slow, deliberate step forward. Lena's breath caught in her throat, and she backed up, her legs weak beneath her. Her fingers tightened around the key, but it felt useless now. There was nowhere to run.

The figure's footfalls were slow, methodical, like it was savoring the moment. Each step seemed to reverberate through the basement, a sharp, echoing sound that made Lena's chest tighten. The closer it got, the more the air seemed to thicken. The room was suffocating, and her mind raced, desperate for answers she knew she might never get.

The figure stopped just a few feet away from her. Lena could see the hollow eyes staring into her, but there was something strange about them. They weren't human. They were too... empty. Like the figure was something that had been lost, a shadow of a person, a hollow shell.

And then, just as Lena's heart threatened to burst out of her chest, the figure smiled.

It was a slow, sickening grin that stretched unnaturally wide, revealing too many teeth, sharp and white against the darkness. The smile didn't seem to belong to the face—it felt like it had been carved there, forcibly, as though the face itself was struggling to contain it.

Lena's breath hitched. Her fingers, still clutching the key, were trembling now, her whole body shaking with fear. "What do you want?" she whispered, though the words barely escaped her throat.

The figure didn't respond. It just stood there, smiling.

And then—just as suddenly as it had appeared—the figure vanished.

Lena blinked, her heart thumping wildly in her chest. The basement was empty. The darkness seemed to press in, but there was no one there. The figure was gone.

For a long moment, Lena didn't move. She couldn't. She stood frozen, unable to comprehend what had just happened. Her eyes scanned the room, the shadows creeping around her like a living thing. She was alone.

But she couldn't shake the feeling that she had just seen

something real. Something that wasn't just a figment of her imagination. The figure—whatever it was—had been there.

And it hadn't come to help her. It had come to warn her.

33

The Haunted Phone

Lena's fingers shook as she held the phone in her hand, the screen flickering intermittently. The darkness of her room seemed to pulse with a strange energy, and she couldn't shake the feeling that the walls were closing in. The air around her felt thick, as though the space itself was holding its breath, waiting for something to happen.

The phone had been silent for hours. And yet, just when she thought she could escape the madness of the basement, the faintest vibration pulsed against her palm. She stared at the screen, feeling her heart leap into her throat as she saw the name that flashed in front of her.

Mom.

Her breath caught in her chest, and for a moment, she thought her mind was playing tricks on her. She knew it couldn't be real. Her mother had died years ago. There was no possible way she could be calling her now, no way that she could be alive again. But the name on the screen was unmistakable.

The phone buzzed again, the call still coming through.

Lena pressed the answer button, her fingers unsteady as she lifted the phone to her ear. Her pulse pounded in her temples, and she felt a chill run down her spine. What was happening? She tried to steady her breath, but her hands were trembling too violently to do so.

The line crackled for a moment, as though it were struggling to find its signal. Then, just as the static cleared, a voice broke through.

"Lena?"

It was soft, tentative, familiar. Her heart skipped.

"Mom?" Her voice broke, the word barely more than a whisper.

For a long moment, there was silence on the other end. Then the voice spoke again, quieter this time, but the words seemed to reverberate in the silence of the room.

"I need you to listen to me. You have to leave. Right now." The words were urgent, panicked, unlike anything Lena remembered from her mother. She felt the hairs on the back of her neck stand up.

"Leave? What—what are you talking about? Where are you? What is going on?" Lena's voice was a mixture of confusion and disbelief. Her heart was hammering now, pounding against her ribcage as she gripped the phone tighter, as if she could physically force an answer from it.

"I don't have much time. You need to go. It's not safe— Lena, please..." The voice on the other end of the line faltered, and for a moment, Lena thought she heard something in the background. A sound. A shuffling noise, like someone moving quickly through a dark space.

Lena's pulse quickened, and she glanced nervously around her room, the shadows too deep and too still. Her room had once been a place of comfort, of memories, but now it felt oppressive, suffocating. It was as though something in the air had changed.

"Mom? What do you mean? Where are you? You're... you're gone." Her throat tightened with the words she didn't want to say, but she couldn't help it. "This isn't possible."

"I know," the voice whispered, and it sounded older, worn out, strained, as if it was fighting to stay coherent. "I'm not the one calling you, Lena. Don't trust it. Don't listen to it."

Lena's breath hitched. The words echoed through her mind. "What do you mean? What's happening?"

The line crackled again, and for a moment, all she could

hear was the sharp static. It sounded distant now, as though the voice on the other end was fading, or being swallowed by something much darker. She pressed the phone harder against her ear, desperate to hear more.

And then, another voice broke through.

The voice was deeper, darker, chilling. It wasn't her mother.

"Well, well, Lena." The voice chuckled low, malicious, as though savoring her confusion. It was smooth, but with an underlying threat. "You didn't think it would be that easy, did you?"

Lena's blood ran cold. The air around her seemed to freeze, and the phone in her hand felt as though it weighed a hundred pounds. She didn't recognize the voice, but it was unmistakably sinister.

"No," Lena whispered, her eyes darting around her room. "No, this isn't real. This isn't happening."

"Oh, it's real, alright," the voice continued, its amusement almost tangible. "You've been following the trail, haven't you? The key, the photo—what do you think all of it means, Lena?"

Her breath caught, and she swallowed hard. The key, the photo in the basement... It all led back to something she hadn't wanted to confront. Something she had been running from.

Lena gripped the phone tighter, her knuckles white. "Who are you?" she demanded, trying to keep her voice steady, but it cracked. "What do you want from me?"

The voice chuckled again, low and menacing. "What do I want? What do you think I want? You've been poking around in places you shouldn't, Lena. You've uncovered things that should've stayed buried. Now, there's no going back."

Lena's heart pounded faster, each beat echoing in her chest. She could feel a cold sweat forming on her skin. "What is this?

Why are you doing this?"

The voice didn't answer at first, but there was a shift in the air around her. She could feel it—a growing presence, something cold and malevolent wrapping itself around her. It was as though the shadows in the corners of the room were pulling closer, inching toward her with every passing second.

Then, the voice returned, this time with a finality that made Lena's stomach drop. "Because it's too late, Lena. You're already a part of it now."

Before Lena could respond, the phone went dead. The line went silent, the call abruptly cut off. She held the phone up, her finger trembling as she stared at the blank screen. The sense of dread that had taken over her body seemed to intensify, every inch of her skin prickling with the weight of unseen eyes.

The house was too quiet.

She looked around again, her breath shallow. She should have called the police, should have done something earlier, but now it felt like it was too late. There was no escaping the truth. Something—someone—was pulling her into a web, and she was tangled in it, stuck in its dark threads.

Lena's mind raced. What had the voice meant when it said she was "already a part of it"? What did they know about her? About her past?

She tried to steady herself, taking deep breaths as she stood. The house felt impossibly still now, too still. The air was suffocating, thick with tension. The shadows seemed deeper than before, pooling in the corners like they were alive, waiting.

And then—just as she was about to turn to leave, the phone buzzed again.

This time, when she looked at the screen, there was no name. No number. Just a string of random letters and symbols, scrolling across the screen like a strange code.

Lena's fingers trembled as she swiped to answer the call, but before she could press the button, the screen went black again.

Her heart raced.

A loud crash echoed from somewhere upstairs, followed by the unmistakable sound of footsteps—slow, deliberate, and heavy.

Lena froze.

9 785518 107380

Printed by Libri Plureos GmbH in Hamburg, Germany